"A thorough and down-to-earth resourc[e] [for anyone pur]suing a legal career. The authors offer valua[ble insights] [to] maximize the reader's success in interview and social situations."

—Howard Armstrong, Partner, Latham & Watkins LLP

"Natalie Prescott and Oleg Cross have produced a volume that will surely fill a need for new law school graduates and experienced attorneys. Plenty of books on the market cover job interviewing, but *Nail Your Law Job Interview* comprehensively explains the nuances of interviewing in the law sector. Mini case-studies and the authors' own experiences enhance their advice. The chapters on timing of law interviews, limiting the disclosure of candidate information in interviews, gap-fillers for awkward moments, and bold moves to help the candidate stand out, provide excellent and little-known information. The authors have clearly thought of—and covered—every contingency that can arise in a law interview, including distinguishing among types of law interviews and types of law positions. No aspiring attorney should be without this book."

—Katharine Hansen, PhD, Associate Publisher/Creative Director of Quintessential Careers, and author of *Top Notch Executive Resumes*

"After surviving law school and the bar exam, many attorneys downplay the difficulty of the job search, and, more specifically, the job interview. In reality, the interview always means the difference between getting passed over and landing your dream job. This book provides candidates with succinct advice, elucidating anecdotes, and inside tips that will allow them to take the guesswork out of the interview process and nail their interviews."

—T.J. Duane, Principal, Lateral Link Group LLC

"This book goes beyond the cookie-cutter guidance found in most other legal job-hunting publications. Its in-depth research and in-the-know, superb 'real world' advice is particularly helpful to candidates interviewing in an increasingly competitive job market."

—Alan D. Surchin, Esq., Executive Recruiter, Pittleman & Associates

"*Nail Your Law Job Interview* is well-written and wonderfully comprehensive. It provides specific examples, directions, and instructions in every aspect of finding a law job. In fact, although it's written for the new grad, experienced lawyers will benefit from it as well. Too many 'how to' books are mostly theory. This one isn't."

—Judi Perkins, "The Renegade Job Coach," founder of Find the Perfect Job, and contributor to Vault.com's career blog

Nail Your Law Job Interview

The Essential Guide to Firm, Clerkship, Government, In-House, and Lateral Interviews

By Natalie Prescott & Oleg Cross

CAREER
PRESS

THE CAREER PRESS, INC.
Pompton Plains, NJ

NAIL YOUR LAW JOB INTERVIEW
EDITED BY KIRSTEN DALLEY
Cover design by Rob Johnson, Johnson Design
Printed in the U.S.A.

To order this title, please call toll-free 1-800-CAREER-1 (NJ and Canada: 201-848-0310) to order using VISA or MasterCard, or for further information on books from Career Press.

The Career Press, Inc., 220 West Parkway, Unit 12
Pompton Plains, NJ 07444
www.careerpress.com

Library of Congress Cataloging-in-Publication Data
Prescott, Natalie.
    Nail your law job interview : the essential guide to firm, clerkship, government, in-house, and lateral interviews / by Natalie Prescott & Oleg Cross.
        p. cm.
    Includes index.
    ISBN 978-1-60163-053-7
        1. Law—Vocational guidance—United States. 2. Practice of law—Vocational guidance—United States. 3. Employment interviewing—United States. I. Cross, Oleg. II. Title.

KF297.P74 2009
650.14'4—dc22
                                                                    2008053974

ACKNOWLEDGMENTS

❧❀❀❧

We owe the success of this book to many legal and recruiting professionals who shared their wisdom and devoted significant time to reviewing and commenting on various chapters. The unique perspectives of many lawyers, judges, law clerks, recruiting coordinators, law students, and legal recruiters helped us shape the contents of this book and transform it into a comprehensive interviewing guide for a diverse group of readers. We are especially grateful to the following people:

To Kate Epstein, Epstein Literary Agency, and Michael Pye and Adam Schwartz of Career Press for believing in and appreciating the importance of this book and for contributing their countless efforts to this project. Thanks also to our editor, Kirsten Dalley, and to Kristen Parkes, who designed the interior of the book.

To the Honorable Roger T. Benitez, U.S. District Court for the Southern District of California, for being such a wonderful mentor and for passing on his knowledge and inspiration during a challenging editorial process.

To Chief Judge Irma E. Gonzalez, U.S. District Court for the Southern District of California; Judge John A. Houston, U.S. District Court for the Southern District of California; Magistrate Judge Cathy A. Bencivengo, U.S. District Court for the Southern District of California; Judge David R. Thompson, U.S. Court of Appeals for the Ninth Circuit; Judge J. Clifford Wallace, U.S. Court of Appeals for the Ninth Circuit; and Judge Barry G. Silverman, U.S. Court of Appeals for the Ninth Circuit, for sharing their knowledge and collective wisdom on the subject of clerkship interviews, which we now pass on to our readers.

To Michael Allen, cofounder of Lateral Link Group LLC; T.J. Duane, principal of Lateral Link Group LLC; Alexis Dixon Johnson, managing director of Major, Lindsey, and Africa, LLC; and Alan Surchin, executive recruiter at Pittleman & Associates, for their invaluable input into a broad array of subjects affecting the lateral market, in-house interviewing process, and tips for using headhunters. Their in-depth knowledge of the intricacies of lateral interviews and the challenges facing lateral candidates helped us gain a deeper understanding of these important subjects.

To Roel C. Campos, partner-in-charge, Cooley Goodward Kronish LLP, and former Commissioner of the U.S. Securities and Exchange Commission; Peter Hyun, Assistant Attorney General, Office of the Attorney General, State of New York; Kim Lagotta, Deputy District Attorney, San Diego County, California, Chief of the Family Protection Unit, and member of the Hiring Evaluation Panel; Elizabeth Porterfield, Deputy District Attorney, San Diego County, California; and Michael Skerlos, Assistant U.S. Attorney for the Southern District of California, and Chair of the Hiring Committee, for their input into the chapter on government interviews.

To Katharine Hansen, author of *Top Notch Executive Resumes*, creative director of Quintessential Careers; Judi Perkins, the "Renegade Job Coach," founder of Find the Perfect Job, recruiter, author, and contributor to Vault.com's career-related blog; Debra Strauss, professor at the Charles F. Dolan School of Business at Fairfield University, author of *Behind the Bench: The Guide to Judicial Clerkships*; and Joe Turner, recruiter, author of *Paycheck 911* and *Job Search Secrets Unlocked*, for their significant written contributions to various chapters in this book, invaluable expertise, and tireless editorial efforts.

To Howard Armstrong, partner and recruiting committee member, Latham & Watkins LLP; Margie Cartwright, Associate Director of Career Services at University of San Diego School of Law; Carlos Davila-Caballero, Assistant Dean for Career Development at Tulane Law School; Bruce Elvin, Director of Career and Professional Development at Duke University School of Law; Cara Mitnick, Assistant Dean for Career Services at University of San Diego School of Law; and Michael G. Rhodes, Litigation Department Chair, and member of the management committee, Cooley Godward Kronish LLP, for fascinating discussions, illuminating interview stories, and feedback regarding law-firm interviews.

To attorneys Elena Bojilova, Jones Day LLP; Albert Chang, law clerk to the Honorable Roger T. Benitez; Kamyar Daneshvar, Bullivant Houser Bailey PC; and Scott McGee, Motley Rice LLC, for spending countless hours reviewing chapters and offering an insider's perspective to the subjects of lateral and callback interviews.

To Katherine Paculba, a recent graduate of the Thomas Jefferson School of Law, for her help with and extensive editing of the networking chapter.

To David Lat, founder of the legal tabloid Abovethelaw.com, for allowing us to draw on the wisdom and experience of his readers in several interview stories throughout this book.

To Jennifer Black, Counsel at Energy Capital Partners; Alice Detwiler, Senior Attorney at Microsoft Corporation; and Stacey Spain, Vice President, Counsel, and Assistant Corporate Secretary at Amback Financial Group, for inspiration, thoughtful discussions, resource materials, and tips on the in-house interviewing process.

To attorneys Brian Brook, Greenberg Traurig LLP; Adam Garson, DLA Piper U.S. LLP; Veronica Jackson, DLA Piper U.S. LLP; Nataliya Johnson, Shook, Hardy & Bacon LLP; Angie Kim, Cooley Godward Kronish LLP; JoAnn Koob, DLA Piper U.S. LLP; Olga May, Fish & Richardson LLP; William Northrip, Shook Hardy & Bacon LLP; and Aryn Thomas, Latham & Watkins LLP, for their edits and thoughtful comments regarding the challenges facing young attorneys interviewing for jobs in a diverse legal market.

To attorneys Stephen Dang, Latham & Watkins LLP; Kiera Gans, DLA Piper U.S. LLP; Tamara Katz, Latham & Watkins LLP; Colin Levere, Clifford Chance LLP; Daina Selvig, DLA Piper U.S. LLP; and Brandee Shtevi, Cooley Godward Kronish LLP, for taking the time to educate us on the unique challenges facing foreign job applicants in the United States, for sharing their stories, and for offering useful tips to our readers.

To Theresa DeLoach, Recruiter at Lateral Link Group LLC; Heather Lodahl, Recruiting Coordinator at Latham & Watkins LLP; Septina McDonnell, Recruiting Manager at Cooley Godward Kronish LLP; and Allison Shanahan, Manager of Attorney Recruitment and Development at Latham & Watkins LLP, for their helpful advice on the law-firm interviewing process.

To current and former clerks Marwan Elrakabawy, Robert Firpo, Joseph Goodman, Erin Goodsell, Sasha Johnson, Christin Hill, Alison Kaisler, Jennifer Kaplan, Michael Leggieri, Katie Lieberg, Robert Newmayer, Jin Ohta, and Glenn Rivera, for their advice, edits, and support.

To the numerous other colleagues, attorneys, students, law schools, and recruiters who have sought advice on job interviews, exchanged ideas, and shared their stories, and who, in doing so, helped us shape the content of this book.

CONTENTS

INTRODUCTION

In today's legal marketplace, good credentials and a polished resume are not enough to get a job, much less keep one. Long gone are the days when a job interview was a pleasant formality, followed by a long, relaxing lunch and a prompt offer of employment. Instead, legal employers scrutinize candidates more carefully, often requiring several rounds of interviews, asking pointed questions, and evaluating interview performance based on a variety of factors ranging from dress code and demeanor to the type of questions they ask.

In addition, the legal profession is becoming increasingly mobile, with most lawyers changing jobs at least once or twice early in their careers. What's more, legal positions are becoming increasingly competitive, as lawyers seek new opportunities due to the economic downturn, layoffs, a need for job security, and/or a quest for better hours. With more choices than ever before, employers have the luxury of demanding that their applicants have precisely the right kind of pedigree and personality fit. They want their hires to be smart, hard-working, entrepreneurial go-getters who will be well-suited to their respective practices, and who will make work their top priority.

In sum, a law degree—no matter how fancy—is no longer a license to print money. Instead, employers expect a candidate to persuade them at the interview why she or he is precisely the right person for the job. By demystifying the interviewing process, this book tells you how to do just that.

An interview is the most important part of the job-search process. It is also the most difficult part. However, similar to any skill, it can be learned and thus performed effectively. Certainly, there are objective hiring criteria that no amount of interviewing skills can transcend. But no legal employer will hire you based on a resume alone. Your credentials and experience will only get you in the door. An interview is what will actually get you the job. Thus, once you get an interview, this book is your most important guide on how to ace it.

The good news is that in most cases, by the time you get to the interviewing table, your credentials have been analyzed, and you have a legitimate shot at the job. But what can you do to ensure you put your best foot forward? The types of questions to ask and to avoid, how to do your homework, whether to use a headhunter, when to write thank-you letters—this book has it all.

We wrote this book because there was a need for a comprehensive interview guide for lawyers transitioning from school or their first job to a successful legal career and beyond. From entry-level to experienced hires, this book answers all interview-related questions. It is a must-read for students and seasoned lawyers alike if they want to improve their interviewing skills prior to interviewing with small or large firms, government employers, judges, or for in-house positions.

Throughout the book, you will discover key issues that commonly arise in most types of legal interviews, as well as some less common successful interviewing techniques. You will also learn from interview stories provided by students, attorneys, judges, and government lawyers. Although all names have been changed, the stories in this book are based on true events.

What you will learn:

✓ Tips and strategies for every kind of law job interview.

✓ How to address weaknesses on your resume and emphasize strengths while still sounding genuine.

✓ How to research and phrase your questions so that they are thoughtful and original.

✓ Ways to distinguish yourself with "bold moves."

✓ The most common mistakes to avoid when trying to make an impression.

✓ How to do your homework.

✓ How to employ flattery without sounding like a stalker.

✓ Techniques for dealing with difficult interview scenarios, arrogant interviewers, and improper or illegal questions.

✓ How to address questions about law, politics, and religion without risking antagonizing your interviewers.

✓ Proper lunch-interview etiquette and casual dress code rules.

✓ Attempts at humor and other interview traps to avoid.

✓ How to position yourself at the interviewing table, what to wear, and what to bring along.

✓ How to write effective thank-you letters, how to negotiate, and questions you should never ask.

✓ Tips for networking, dealing with rejection, and interviewing after getting fired.

✓ Advice for scheduling and timing your on-campus, lateral, and clerkship interviews in a way that can increase your chances of receiving an offer.

✓ Real-life examples of effective interview techniques and common pitfalls, provided by students, attorneys, and judges.

✓ How to address specific interview scenarios throughout your career.

·✓ Short chapter summaries for when you are on the go.

After interviewing hundreds of legal professionals, including law firm recruiters, headhunters, hiring partners, judges, top government attorneys, and in-house counsel, we included their advice and perspectives in the chapters for candidates interviewing in their respective fields. Their collective wisdom, real-life examples from both sides of the interviewing table, and our advice and experience give you all the tools needed to *nail your law job interview.*

Part I

❧❀❧

Getting Started

Chapter 1

How to Network With Ease

Learning to network is crucial to your career. Yet networking has somehow become a dirty word. While many self-proclaimed experts preach the importance of networking, they rarely explain what it entails. Instead, they make networking sound so difficult that people feel overwhelmed and resentful about having to network. Admittedly, networking is not easy, but it is not impossible to master. This chapter is your guide to networking with ease. It is short and easy to follow. First, it demystifies the process; then it offers effective shortcuts to successful networking. Put simply, networking is the process of making, retaining, and using contacts.

Making Contacts: Always Be on the Lookout

You will be amazed at how many contacts you can gather once you make an effort. From the first day of law school and throughout your career you will meet countless professors, guest speakers, distinguished alumni, attorneys, and members of the state and federal judiciary. Even your fellow classmates are an invaluable networking resource: Many of them may become your clients, colleagues, or supervisors.

Networking happens everywhere, from bar events and charity auctions to internal law firm events that lawyers attend for the CLE (Continuing Legal Education) credits and free food. So what can you do to make sure you network effectively? First, do attend these events. If you are a student with a demanding schedule, try to attend as many as you can. If you think your schedule is busy now, just wait until you start working! If you are an attorney, attending these events may cost more, so attend as many as your schedule permits and as many as your employer will reimburse you for.

Second, when you attend these events, make sure you actually talk to people you do not know. It may be terrifying at first, but it will get easier. Even the most outspoken, outgoing people are intimidated when they are forced to introduce themselves to a bunch of seasoned lawyers or judges.

Most young lawyers do not make enough of an effort to walk around the room and introduce themselves, let alone regard these people as future contacts. This translates into time and opportunity wasted. If you have recently looked at your tuition or student loan statements, you can see that the cost of this opportunity is substantial.

Third, recognize that every speaker, alumna/alumnus, and practitioner you meet is a contact who could help you with employment or other opportunities in the future. Remember, your current job is probably not the last job you will ever have, and knowing people helps if you ever need to make a move. Memorize their names, retain their contact information, and call upon them in your time of need.

Fourth, when you have an opportunity to meet a potential contact, embrace it. Introduce yourself. Rather than doing all the talking, ask questions. Soak up the information like a sponge. Lawyers love talking about themselves, so your contacts will have no problem discussing their careers and achievements. Ask them about their jobs and why they do what they do. Discuss their presentations, community involvement, or anything else of relevance. Your conversation may be informative but not deeply personal—it may even feel superficial—but that is to be expected. Even if your encounter is very brief, and your contact doesn't fully remember you in the future, your main goal is to have a personal interaction. Get some face time, relax, and enjoy the conversation.

Fifth, realize that networking is unlikely to produce immediate results. Instead of focusing on short-term goals, you should concentrate on building goodwill. Lawyers, judges, and clients may remember you favorably years down the road simply because you had engaging conversations in the past. When you network, you want to collect these people—people who later may want to see you succeed—in your personal net. When the right time comes, you may be able to rely on their support or expertise.

Finally, remember that this is a small world. Consequently, you may be networking even when you are not aware of it. The person next in line in a grocery store or next to you in church may be a judge or a lawyer. Always be friendly and courteous to others.

Amy learned from her mistakes. One day, she was taking the subway to a job interview, and a woman standing next to her accidentally tore Amy's pantyhose with her purse. Amy was beyond angry, and she exploded into a passive-aggressive rant. But when she proceeded to exit the train, Amy discovered that the "offender" was getting off at the same station. To her horror, the woman was heading to the same building as Amy. She was one of Amy's interviewers! Amy apologized for her emotional outburst, but, of course, she did not get an offer.

Retaining Contacts

Your contacts will be useless if you forget about them. Do not let that happen. Ideally, you should create a written or electronic record of every contact you have made. You can do this on your BlackBerry, PalmPilot, Excel spreadsheet, or in an old-fashioned address book. Create categories for the person's name and position, as well as for the location, date, and description of the conversation. Shortly after you meet someone who could be even remotely useful to you, make a corresponding entry.

And, because you may never follow this advice due to lack of time, here is a shortcut: Collect business cards you receive from your contacts and jot down a few relevant notes on the back of each one. Sure this sounds a bit stalkerish, but it can be highly effective. When you are applying for a fellowship or switching jobs a year or two later, or when your client needs legal advice from an experienced practitioner, you can rely on your contact list to find help. Initiate your contact via e-mail to give him or her enough time to remember you (or at least to Google you). You can begin your e-mail with something along these lines: "My name is ___. I am writing to you because we met at ___, where we discussed ___. I was very impressed with your ___. When I was considering ___, I thought of you and our conversation."

Even if your contact has absolutely no recollection of the meeting, he or she will be flattered you remembered him or her. Therefore, retain the information about your contacts and store it in an organized manner. One day it will come in handy. The bottom line is that if you do not find a way to preserve contact information, you will never be able to use it.

Finally, be patient; gaining good networking contacts does not happen overnight. Do not be overly aggressive and do not try to use your contacts too soon. You will eventually discover that the people who are most generous with their time and knowledge are those you have met over the course of many events or even years. If you pounce on your contacts after the first or second meeting, they will likely hold you at arms-length. Meanwhile, if you take the time to build a long-term relationship with them, they will be more eager to help you.

Using Your Contacts Wisely

This is perhaps the trickiest part of this three-pronged approach. Lawyers are often bombarded with e-mails and phone calls from students from their alma mater or even random, off-the-street job-seekers, asking for help with employment. During our very first year as associates at large firms, we received dozens of such unsolicited messages. We encourage you not to perpetuate this trend. If you must use your contacts before you develop a relationship with them, be subtler and less aggressive in your communications. There are two acceptable ways of doing this.

First, you can e-mail your contact with a request for a brief informational interview. Seek information or advice, but do not ask for too much; and definitely do not ask for a job. A request like this can be effective because it is flattering to your contact; it implies that he or she is an expert, and that his or her opinion and time are valuable. Additionally, it only asks for a few minutes of his or her time, which makes it more difficult for him or her to say no. Finally, it requires minimal effort to respond. Just remember to stick to your promise to keep the conversation brief, unless you are encouraged to ask more questions. Here is an acceptable format for this request:

> "My name is ____, and I am a second-year law student at ____. I am writing to you because we met at ____ a few months ago where we discussed ____. I am seeking some information about ____. Given your expertise in this area, I was wondering if I could have a few minutes of your time to discuss this topic. I realize that, as a practicing attorney, you have a very busy schedule. However, I would really appreciate hearing your thoughts on this topic. Thank you in advance for your time."

Second, you can mail your employment application packet to this person. As long as you are not asking for an actual response, this method of contacting your networking contact is appropriate and not invasive. Such an inquiry does not obligate your contact to commit much time, nor does it ask for any favors. Your contact may either ignore your application or—if you are lucky—help you get an interview.

The most effective method of using your contacts is to seek out ways to help them. Networking often has a negative connotation because it is sometimes equated with using others. But, in reality, networking is about give and take, and the most effective networkers are not only users but also givers. Next time, do not be that person who only calls when they need something. Instead of cruising a cocktail room searching for someone who can potentially help you, consider how you can help them. You will be surprised at how much you have to offer. Volunteering for someone's law committee, sending your contacts interesting articles, helping them put materials together for presentations, collaborating on pro bono projects, contributing to a publication, introducing your contacts to people with similar interests, or simply being visibly loyal to your contacts can all be effective networking tools!

Finally, remember to thank people who helped you. If your contact goes out of his or her way to do something for you, it is crucial that you go out of your way to thank this person. Consider sending a handwritten note, and a nice thank-you e-mail or card for small favors, and flowers or a gift basket for big favors. It will go a long way, especially if you need this person's help again in the future.

This is the simple guide to networking. In a nutshell, if you are willing to go out there and meet new people, you have already accomplished half of the difficult task. Do not forget to retain information about your contacts and actually use your contacts in the future. Happy networking!

QuickReview

✓   Do not let your fear of networking stop you from meeting new people.

✓   Attend events, meetings, and attorney gatherings whenever you can.

✓   Remember that networking is a two-way street.

✓   Treat every contact as an invaluable resource.

✓   Always be courteous and polite to everyone—your paths may cross in the future.

✓   Develop a system for retaining your contacts, and write down relevant information about the people you have met.

✓   Saying something flattering to your contact can go a long way.

✓   Ask for little and you will receive a great deal.

Chapter 2

TIMING IS EVERYTHING

⟨∞⟩

You may be surprised to learn that a such seemingly minor factor as the timing of a job interview can have a major impact on your success. Interviewees normally do not obsess about timing in the same way they do about resumes, dress codes, or interview questions. Meanwhile, interviewers are very responsive to timing issues. When scheduling your interviews, make the timing work to your advantage.

When to Arrive

Never be late for an interview. Arrive 10 to 20 minutes early to ensure you are at the right place, to avoid being late, and to give yourself more face time. During on-campus interviews, for example, interviews sometimes end early, which can present you with a golden opportunity to spend extra time with the interviewer. However, do not knock before your time comes. The interviewer may be taking a few minutes to make a phone call or to finish evaluating the previous candidate. When your time comes, knock on the door decisively. If there is no answer, wait for a few minutes before knocking again. Usually, you will receive a response after the first or the second knock. There are exceptions, however.

Holly once interviewed with a partner who was so full of himself that he did not even bother to respond to her knocks. First, she knocked at her scheduled time—there was no answer. She then waited for several minutes before knocking again—still no answer. Yet she could clearly hear the voices behind the door. A full 10 minutes of her 20-minute interview had passed, and the interviewer still did not acknowledge Holly. She knocked the third time—once again, still no answer. At that point, Holly did not know what to do. The school's interview manual did not account for unresponsive partners who required more than three knocks. She felt it was inappropriate to knock again and thought about leaving; however, out of curiosity she stayed. Several minutes later the interviewer finally emerged. He neither apologized nor acknowledged his unresponsiveness. Nevertheless, Holly conducted herself in a respectful manner and received a callback—which she did not accept.

When to Schedule

Morning interviews are more likely to start on time, and are less likely to be interrupted or canceled due to client emergencies. In the first half of the day, your interviewers will be less tired, and your presentation will be more effective because your head, attire, and coffee are still fresh. Accordingly, try to schedule your interviews early.

For on-campus interviews, do not schedule back-to-back interviews because you will almost certainly end up being late to your second interview. Additionally, try to schedule interviews with your top-choice firms early in the morning and before your interviews with your "safety" firms. During on-campus interviews, your chances of getting an offer may be higher if you interview earlier in the day. In the morning, the interviewers are alert, they pay more attention, and they have not yet made up their minds about which candidates to give callbacks to. So, if they like you, you could be the person whose resume goes in the callback pile. You had better hope your classmates are not reading this chapter carefully!

Here is why this advice makes sense: An employer typically comes on campus with a certain number of callback offers at hand. Usually, the firm will give callbacks to one to three students from a given school after a day of interviews. Early in the day, this quota is not yet filled, so your chances of being "the one" are significantly higher. The later in the day it gets, the more you have to impress your interviewer to get a callback. It is like watching a circus for 12 hours straight. You had better throw in some cool magic tricks at the end of the show if you want to dazzle your audience. This is not to say you will not get an offer if you interview later in the day; you just may have to work harder for it.

What do you do if you or your interviewer is not a morning person? Only you know what works best for you. So if you perform better later in the day, by all means schedule your interviews then. If you notice that your interviewer is having trouble staying awake, invite him or her to grab a cup of coffee, and you will get a chance for a more informal interviewing experience. Be sure to read Chapter 13 to see how to pull this off.

Callback Interviews: The Sooner the Better

When you receive a callback, make sure to call the firm's recruiter and schedule the interview as soon as possible. Many people prefer to wait for weeks or even months so they can group their out-of-town interviews together. We do not recommend this approach. Firms usually make offers on a rolling basis; just as they do during on-campus interviews, they have a quota to fill. They tend to be more generous with offers earlier in the interviewing season than toward the end of the season. Consequently, your chances increase (even if slightly) by interviewing early. Furthermore, firms can schedule only a limited number of callbacks on any given day because callbacks require a great deal of manpower. If you do not schedule your interview early, you may be interviewing at an inconvenient time, your callback may be pushed toward the end of the recruiting season, or it may even be canceled.

> Carla waited until the last minute to schedule her callback interviews. When she finally called to schedule them, one firm had already filled all the openings and was no longer hiring, and several others asked her to fly for callbacks merely days before the NALP deadline for accepting offers. As a result, she ended up missing out on these interviews.

Lateral Interviews: The Earlier the Better

Lateral candidates are usually given more flexibility when it comes to scheduling interviews. Because they have other work commitments, potential employers attempt to be courteous and accommodating. In fact, some firms even ask whether candidates prefer breakfast, lunch, dinner, or cocktails for an interview "meal." Additionally, firms do not usually hold it against a candidate if he or she has to reschedule an interview, as long as it does not happen more than once. The same is not true for in-house interviews, however. Never cancel an in-house interview once you have scheduled it!

When scheduling lateral interviews, remember that interviewing in the morning is best. Accordingly, if you are given a choice, choose breakfast over lunch and lunch over dinner for an interview. Breakfast is the best choice because it feels festive and relaxing, people are usually in less of a hurry, and the interviewers seem somewhat happier than usual thanks to an unlimited supply of freshly brewed coffee. Lunch is also good, although people tend to eat in a hurry. Dinner is generally a bad choice, because your interviewers are being forced to take the time away from their families and friends in order to attend a dinner with you. There is a chance they may subconsciously resent you for this. Why take the risk? Finally, drinks are downright bad, so resist the temptation.

Clerkship Interviews: First Come, First Served

At the beginning of the clerkship interviewing season, judges call candidates on a rolling basis. Some judges extend the courtesy of not making offers until they meet all of the candidates. Other judges make offers on the spot because they are concerned that the good candidates will be snatched away. It is not uncommon, for example, for a judge who offered you an interview to call back and inform you that all positions have been filled before you even had a chance to meet the judge. Therefore, if you are lucky enough to receive a clerkship interview, try to meet the judge as soon as possible.

With regard to timing of the interviews, most likely you will not be given the privilege of choosing the time of the day. Instead, much as it is with court appearances, you will be told when to appear and present yourself. Some judges are notorious for interviewing candidates at odd hours; we have heard of clerkship interviews scheduled as late as midnight. Others interview candidates between the hours of 6 and 7 a.m. Of course, you shouldn't turn down an interview simply because it is scheduled at an odd hour. So, take whatever time you can get, be courteous, and thank the judge profusely for making the time to see you. Then, by all means, make it to the interview at the time the judge requested, even if it means missing your own wedding. Just do not do what one student did. She called the chambers to inform the judge's secretary that she had a class during the time when the judge wanted to interview her, and that she wanted to reschedule her interview to a "more convenient time." That more convenient time never came.

If this chapter has a theme, it is that earlier is better. This is true for all types of interviews. Whether you interview as a law student, a lateral, or a clerkship candidate, the same rule applies. All job vacancies function on the dynamic of supply and demand, and interviewing later means someone may beat you to the punch. With callback and lateral interviews, interviewing earlier in the day also makes your interview more enjoyable and productive because your interviewers are not as tired or busy as they will be later in the day. Finally, scheduling interviews with your top-choice employers first means you may receive your top-choice offer before having to interview with your second- and third-choice employers.

QuickReview

✓ Given a choice, always try to schedule your interviews earlier in the day.

✓ Try not to schedule your on-campus interviews back to back.

✓ Employers can only give out a limited number of offers, and those candidates who interview early have a greater chance of success.

✓ Schedule interviews with your top-choice employers first.
✓ Unless there are compelling reasons why you cannot make it, take
   the first available clerkship interview opportunity.

Chapter 3

HOW TO DO YOUR HOMEWORK

Doing your homework is important, especially during callbacks, small-firm, and government interviews. Never interview "cold." Even during initial interviews, you must know a substantial amount about the employer and the interviewer. This chapter tells you how to prepare for all kinds of interviews by doing research, anticipating questions, and finding common conversation topics.

Educate Yourself About Practice Areas

Firms often do different types of work in different offices. When your interviewer asks, "Why do you want to join us?" or "What type of work are you interested in doing?" you should be able to articulate something better than "Your firm has a great reputation." If you have a specific interest in, say, Russian capital markets or international arbitration, it may be useful to know whether the firm's Phoenix office (in which you have indicated a strong interest) does that sort of thing. At the callback stage, there is no greater threat to your offer than not knowing what your interviewer and his or her colleagues do.

> Brian was interested in Asia/Pacific Rim work and Islamic finance—both, no doubt, interesting and rewarding practices in which some attorneys at this firm could have specialized. Unfortunately, these attorneys did not work in the office where Brian was applying. The interviewer's immediate reaction was, "Why are you here? Shouldn't you be interviewing with some other office or a firm that does that?"

Your interviewers should not have to explain to you what their firm does, especially at the callback stage. This is especially true for small-firm and government positions. Most of the time, this information is publicly available online. Even if you have little time, spend at least a few minutes on Google and on the firm's Website prior to the interview to ensure that you are familiar with the firm's practice areas and your interviewers. Never leave your interviewers with a feeling that they just wasted precious, otherwise billable time on reciting publicly available information.

Transactional vs. Litigation

Most small firms either specialize in a narrow field, or practice an "eat what you kill" appraoch and work on a wide variety of cases. Meanwhile, large firms departmentalize. Know precisely what the firm's practice areas are.

Most medium and large firms consist of at least two major departments: transactional and litigation. The practice groups in a transactional department may include merger and acquisition work, private equity, and real estate transactions; in litigation, they may include employment, securities, product liability, intellectual property, and insurance. What you need to know for now is this: transactional lawyers draft contracts, help structure deals, advise clients on specific transactions, and, invariably, perform due diligence. Litigators, on the other hand, primarily write briefs, memos, and motions; research the law; review documents; and attend depositions and, occasionally, make court appearances.

For every transaction gone sour, there is a litigator who will either take someone to court or make a buck defending a lawsuit. Transactional and litigation work require different sets of skills. If you are interviewing while in law school or soon after graduation, you have not yet developed either of these skill sets. So, for the purposes of on-campus and callback interviews, simply know what the firm does and what your interests are, and try to pick one of the two areas.

If you are torn between these choices or feel uncertain about your interests, consider this advice: People who enjoy and/or do well in subjects such as contracts, business associations, and bankruptcy, and classes that require an understanding and memorization of rules and statutes, often discover they have a preference for transactional work. Meanwhile, law students who like subjects such as torts, product liability, constitutional law, criminal law, and legal research and writing, often lean toward litigation. But keep in mind that these are broad generalizations.

For the purposes of interviewing, try to make a choice sooner rather than later. You do not have to commit to it forever; plenty of young attorneys change their minds and switch from one practice area to another during the first few years of practice. Saying, "I haven't had a chance to explore different specialties, but right now I am leaning towards X" is much better than saying, "I do not know what I want to do."

Furthermore, demonstrate realistic expectations about your future job, or the employers will see you as a flight risk. For example, if an interviewer at a medium or large firm asks you why you want to be a litigator, an answer such as "I enjoy research and writing" will fare better than "I would like to spend my days in court." This is because court appearances are difficult to come by for associates at larger firms. Meanwhile, when interviewing at small firms, indicate your willingness to take on significant responsibility early in your career, and your desire to attend court appearances and obtain trial experience. This is important because small firms seek people who are self-starters and who are not afraid of responsibility.

If you are interested in corporate work at a large firm, stating "I want to work on large sophisticated deals" will leave a better impression than "I'm a good negotiator." Likewise, telling your interviewers that the firm will benefit from your language skills and cross-cultural experiences is better than saying you "want to practice international law." Candidates who want to practice international law without clear understanding of what such a practice involves can be an interviewer's biggest pet peeve.

Pick an Area

At the callback stage with larger firms, the firm's recruiter may ask you about your interests in certain practice areas, so that he or she can arrange interviews with attorneys who do that type of work. Even though you may feel forced to commit to a practice area before you have actually had a chance to figure out what you want to do, brush off this feeling. Again, you will have plenty of time to choose a practice area during your work as a summer associate and in the early stages of your career. Right now, you simply must exhibit some decisiveness and the ability to commit.

> While scheduling a callback interview with a summer associate candidate, Tammy, a recruiting coordinator, asked whether he was interested in corporate law or litigation. The question was of particular significance because the firm's litigation and corporate offices were in two opposite parts of town. The candidate thought about this question for a long time while Tammy waited, but he just could not decide. Tammy ultimately had to schedule interviews at both offices, which meant the candidate had to take a cab across town after his second interview, fight mid-afternoon traffic, miss his interview lunch, and inconvenience the interviewers' schedules. His inability to make a choice cost him an offer.

When interviewing with small firms, however, your desire to do the type of work the firm does is more important than your ability to pick a specialty. In fact, small firms often prefer candidates who can practice in diverse areas rather than those who want to zero in on one area (unless this is the one area the firm specializes in).

Sources of Information

There are numerous resources that can provide you with more than enough information for your interviews: the employer's Website, the NALP directory, the Vault.com guide, Martindale-Hubble, information gathered by law-school career services, newspaper articles, and employers' press releases and publications. Consider using one or two but not all of them, as that will likely overwhelm you and prove to be too time consuming. If you have more time, you may find entertaining tips on Websites such as *www.law.com*, *www.abovethelaw.com*, and *www.lawyerconfessions.com*. These Websites offer interesting discussions on such topics as firm scandals, compensation issues, and lateral moves, to name a few.

For firm interviews, you should always turn to the firm's Website first. It is the best source of information because it has links to practice areas and attorneys' profiles. Reviewing this information will help you determine whether the firm really has a strong practice in a certain area, or it is simply listing it in hopes of growing in that area. The NALP directory at *www.nalpdirectory.com* is another great source of information. It is particularly useful to quickly assess the size of an office, the number of attorneys in each of the firm's departments, the name of the hiring partner, the recruiting person's contact information, and the number of summer associates.

For small firms, which sometimes do not have Websites, begin your research by consulting the attorney profiles on Martindale-Hubble. Once you figure out who these attorneys are and what they do, Google them. Consult state-bar Websites as well, which may list basic background information about these attorneys. Finally, research the attorneys and the firm on Westlaw or Lexis to find out about cases in which they have been involved. Although this process can be time-consuming, it is still the best way to research small firms.

For government interviews, you should review information available online, paying particular attention to recent cases on which your interviewers may have worked. Also take a look at the agency's Website, newsletters, and a job description, if there is one. Talk to people who have worked there in the past or are currently working there, because they can also be a great source of information. Finally, *www.vault.com* provides useful information on various government jobs.

For clerkship interviews, start by researching the judge on Google. Then, review recent opinions and articles authored by the judge. Also take a look at Martindale-Hubble and the Almanac of the Federal Judiciary. Find out about the judge's background, nomination, and anything particularly interesting about him or her. Ask former clerks and your law-school career services for feedback about the judge. Finally, if you have time, read *Behind the Bench: The Guide to Judicial Clerkships* by Debra Strauss. This book offers excellent advice about clerkships in general, and interviews in particular.

For in-house interviews, you may find the following resources helpful: the American Corporate Counsel Association, *www.acca.com*; the National Law Journal, *www.nlj.com*; *www.law.com* (look for the newsletters targeting in-house attorneys); The In-House Blog, *www.inhouseblog.com*; *Corporate Counsel Magazine*, *www.corpcounsel.com*; and the book *America's Greatest Places to Work with a Law Degree*, by Kimm Alayne Walton.

The Interviewer's Biography

Knowing the facts about the interviewer can have its perks.

> Charlotte once noticed that her interviewer listed gourmet cooking as one of his hobbies on the firm's Website. It so happened that Charlotte had an interest in that area as well. Knowing about the interviewer's passion, Charlotte brought up gourmet cooking during the interview. Their previously dry conversation took a pleasant turn to a discussion about Northern Italian cuisine. Charlotte got a callback the next day.

Your level of research and preparation will vary. During on-campus interviews, you may get away with knowing just the basics—the firm's profile, the interviewer's name, where he or she went to law school and undergrad, and any other interesting information listed on the firm's Website. During callbacks and lateral interviews, however, you are expected to know more. Of course, if you are very interested in a job, be thoroughly prepared.

If you are interviewing with a small firm that does not have a Website (which is rare), or if you just want to know the basics about your interviewer's bio, you can consult Martindale-Hubble, a reliable lawyer locator, which contains the basic facts about credentials, practice areas, and contact information. It is fine to conduct a basic search, but know enough about your interviewer not to ask the obvious questions. Do not ask where he or she went to school or what his or her practice area is. You are expected to know this.

On the other hand, if you are well-prepared, be careful not to sound like a stalker. Although it is a good idea to Google your interviewer, do not ask him or her about personal details (trips, children, and so on). If, for example, you read an article by your interviewer in which he relates that he is a cat lover, you may not want to ask him about his cats just yet.

Before he realizes where you obtained this information, he may feel a little uneasy about your knowledge of such personal details. Ideally, you will find a way to strike up a conversation about cats without admitting you know about his interests. Just be careful not to pry, and never recite any facts that your interviewer may find embarrassing.

> Lynda once interviewed a senior partner for an in-house position at Lynda's company. The partner's preparedness impressed Lynda, and she was flattered when the partner revealed that she researched Lynda online. But when the partner mentioned that she found Lynda's photo on a certain blog, Lynda couldn't help but feel embarrassed. She instantly realized that the photo was a risqué picture of her from her younger days. For the rest of the interview, Lynda was thinking about the embarrassing photo instead of focusing on her interviewee.

Doing your homework about your interviewer is important, but presenting it in the right way is crucial. Occasional flattery is appreciated; open, persistent compliments, done for the sake of getting an offer, are not. So, by all means, talk about your interviewer and flatter him or her, but sound genuine.

Anticipate Common Questions

We will not give you a laundry list of the common interview questions; it will not help you prepare. Questions will vary greatly from one employer to another; those that are repeated are, frankly, not the best questions. A good interviewer should ask you questions that are uniquely tailored to your background, resume, and skills. Clichéd questions do not accomplish this goal. Moreover, you can easily anticipate common questions yourself. For example, you probably know that your interviewer is likely to ask "What makes you a strong candidate for this job?" or "Why do you want to work here?"

Practice answering questions before your interviews, and be a storyteller. Think in advance about the events in your life that made you who you are. Think about how these events influenced your career path, gave you a desire to practice law, or made you a better lawyer. Then, if asked a question about your skills, background, or career choices, tell a story. Stories are much more engaging and convincing than dry answers. Remember to focus on the key points on your resume, and use your background and credentials as leverage.

Know Current Events

Interview questions about politics, sports, and news are rare. But they do come up, especially if there is something in your background to trigger them. If you are from New England, for example, you may have to talk about a recent Patriots game. You may have to discuss basketball if you are a Dukie. If you are from Southern California, your interviewer may ask about wildfires. Or he or she may inquire if your family is safe after a hurricane in Florida. If you were born overseas, you may have to discuss current political issues in your home country. The possibilities are endless.

The best way to prepare for such questions is by staying abreast of current events, determining what interesting parts of your background may trigger questions, and brushing up on sports. We recently consulted with a candidate named Kathleen on her upcoming interview in San Diego. We told her to read about a recent Chargers game; because the Chargers were having a great season, we knew that at least one of her interviewers would likely mention them. And mention them they did! The advice came in handy, as Kathleen knew virtually nothing about sports. She was able to learn enough information beforehand to carry on a meaningful conversation.

Research Yourself

In addition to researching your employers, remember to Google yourself before the interview. Be prepared to deal with any questionable, inappropriate, or scandalous entries linked to your name; if necessary, contact Internet providers and ask them to remove your name and/or photograph from their Websites. Make sure any personal Websites, blogs, and photographs posted online look professional. Finally, if you cannot delete damaging information, be prepared to address it during your interview and explain why you still deserve an offer.

Educating yourself about practice areas and the interviewer's background will take some time and research. Although you do not have to memorize clients' names or newsworthy cases by heart, it is important to understand what type of work is done in the office where you are applying, and what your interviewer does. Consult various sources of information before your interview, research the interviewers' bios and the employer's Website, and anticipate questions.

QuickReview

✓ Research the employer, the interviewer, and information about yourself on the Web.

✓ Know at least the basics about your interviewer's background, be aware of the firm's practice areas, and know what the attorneys at a particular office do.

✓   Do not be indecisive when asked about what you want to do.

✓   Pick several similar areas of interest and be prepared to explain why you are interested in them.

✓   Do not overemphasize your interest in a practice area in which your potential employer may lack expertise.

✓   Research your interviewers' bios and mention relevant facts during your interviews.

✓   Brush up on current events, sports, and politics.

Chapter 4

WHAT TO BRING

ᘓᕈᘏ

What you bring with you into the interviewing room is just as important as your appearance and your answers. Yet, many people focus solely on appearance and preparation while forgetting to pay attention to what they carry. What you bring with you should communicate that you are professional, confident, and well-prepared, and provide ready "take-aways" for busy interviewers. Your packet or portfolio should consist of a manila folder, your resume, a short writing sample, transcripts, and a list of references. After you finish putting these materials together, do not forget to print your name on the folder so it is clearly visible. As a finishing touch for on-campus interviews, you can clip on a passport-sized photo of yourself on the inside cover. Your school may even offer complimentary folders with the school logo on the cover, which are perfect for this occasion. Finally, if you want to look professional during your interviews, you must leave all of your extraneous stuff behind. Items such as large bags, drinks, and cell phones are distracting and rude.

The Packet

Your packet or portfolio accomplishes three goals: it makes you look good, it educates the interviewer about your candidacy, and it helps the interviewer remember who you are. The vast majority of legal interviews happen during a very short time period, with a large number of candidates interviewing for the same position. Faced with such an abundance of applicants, employers often have a difficult time putting together names and faces after a long day of interviews. The materials in your packet will help you make a lasting impression on your interviewers.

Preparing these packets can be somewhat time consuming and costly, but it is important to have one available for each of your interviewers. At a minimum, you should have enough for your top-choice employers (for on-campus interviews), or for the hiring partner and the recruiting coordinator (for callback and lateral interviews). This will ensure that your portfolio is available to everyone on the hiring committee.

If you have a business card, include it in your packet, as well. Judi Perkins, a job coach and a cofounder of Find Your Perfect Job, recommends investing in "bio" business cards. In addition to your name and contact information, these cards should list several salient aspects of your job search (specialty, experience, targeted positions, and so on). Because people are sometimes more likely to retain business cards than packets of information or resumes, a bio card may remind them to contact you about a last-minute job opening or an interview.

Resume

Whether or not you bring packets to your interviews, always have extra copies of your updated resume and transcripts on hand. Employers often ask for them at an interview, and you will look unprepared if you cannot produce them on the spot.

Some candidates also wonder whether they should spend extra money on fancy paper. Most interviewers agree that nice resume paper has no bearing on their decision to interview or hire a candidate. Instead of investing in designer paper, take the time to proofread your resume, correct errors, and organize it better. A well-written and well-organized resume will impress your interviewers much more than a poorly edited resume on scented paper.

Judicial clerks, who sort through hundreds of resumes of "wannabe" clerks in the fall, will tell you that no matter how stellar your grades or how impeccable your credentials are, they will always trash an application with typos in it. Likewise, all legal employers frown on poorly written resumes.

> One student did not receive a callback because he listed "pubic service" (instead of "public service") on his resume. Another student's application was on its way to the judge's chambers when the clerk discovered several typos on an otherwise strong resume. Upon discovering the typos, the clerk threw away this application—one of only 10 selected for interviews.

Writing Samples

Your packet should include your writing samples. However, even if you managed to get an article published, please do not bring a copy of the journal. At best, employers will find it cumbersome, lengthy, and unhelpful;

at worst, they will find it arrogant. Instead, include five to 10 pages from your article, together with a cover page explaining that it was accepted for publication or recently published in a certain journal.

Your writing sample should rarely exceed 10 pages. No matter how brilliant your 50-page *magnum opus* may be, no employer will appreciate having to carry it around or having to flip through it to find your best writing. If you prefer to use a longer piece, you should prepare a 10-page excerpt of it. Interviewers will typically only evaluate the first few paragraphs of your sample, if they choose to look at it at all. So make sure your introduction is clear and concise, and contains no use of the passive voice or long sentences. Have other people proofread it more than once.

A partner at a major firm related to us that he once interviewed a student from a very good school. The student had great credentials, the interview went well, and the partner really liked him and had already decided to give him an offer. However, during his flight home, he thought he would kill some time by reading the writing samples of the candidates he interviewed that day. This particular student's sample was written fairly well, but it had several poorly worded sentences, misspellings, and three punctuation errors on the very first page. From that moment, the partner no longer considered this student for an offer. He explained to us that a good writer must be diligent, and that there was a greater risk that this particular student would continue to produce sloppy work once he joined the firm.

Because your credentials take priority, a good writing sample may not affect the employer's decision; however, a typo or a misplaced comma in your sample will jeopardize an offer.

Finally, remember your ethical obligations. Do not present a writing sample that was edited by someone else as your original work. If you use a memo from your previous job, remember to redact it by deleting confidential information. Instead of using a black marker, we recommend redacting by using a clearly fictitious name, by using X symbols to replace identifying information, or by using a made-up name along with a footnote explaining the change. It is also a good idea to obtain permission from your prior employer when you use their work product, to indicate if your sample is "unedited," and to list this information in a footnote or a cover letter attached to the writing sample.

Transcripts

You should always have extra copies of transcripts with you. Employers ask for them all the time, and they expect you to bring them to an interview. Although you should include your law school transcripts in your packet, consider making your undergraduate transcripts available, as well, especially if you do not yet have law school grades or if your undergraduate transcripts are much more impressive than those from law school.

If you do not have an official transcript yet, it is acceptable to submit an unofficial version in the form of a printout of your academic profile. Just make sure you indicate that it is not an official transcript, and let the employer know that you will forward them an actual transcript as soon as it becomes available. Just be aware that this option can sometimes put you at a disadvantage.

> When Mark interviewed for a summer associate position at a large firm, he provided a sloppy typed transcript to his interviewers. That same day, however, one of his classmates also interviewed with this firm. This classmate handed in an official transcript to the same interviewer who had met Mark earlier that day. According to this interviewer, Mark's "unofficial" transcript was the reason he did not get an offer. The firm decided he was either not diligent enough or, even worse, dishonest. They did not bother to find out.

References

Having a list of references becomes less important the more senior you become in your legal career. It is most important, however, for first-year law students, government attorney candidates, and clerkship applicants. Most of the time, these particular candidates have little or no relevant experience, and potential employers tend to rely on references to assess their abilities.

Lateral candidates are often asked to submit a list of references once they have received and accepted an offer. If you are interviewing as a lateral, you can ask the firms to treat your application as confidential and not contact your references without your prior permission. This is necessary because most firms require references from your current employer, which may be in the dark about you interviewing. The firm where you are interviewing will usually honor your request and refrain from contacting your references until you actually accept their conditional offer of employment.

In general, it is a good idea to have a list of references in your packet. Although very few employers will actually bother to call all the people on your list, many will be delighted to see that you have a list prepared at the interview stage. You should list the names of three people, as well as their e-mail addresses, telephone numbers, and job titles. If you are still in law school or if you graduated recently, you can list your law professors who know you well. Of course, you should not list family members or friends as your references. If you can obtain letters of recommendation, consider doing it instead of or in addition to listing references.

Most importantly, make sure you ask your references whether you can share their contact information. The last thing you want is for a potential employer to call someone on your list of references, only to find out that the person does not remember you or does not have anything meaningful to say about you.

What Not to Bring

Interviewees who carry large loads of stuff to the interviews may appear less professional and less organized than those who manage to leave the heavy weight behind. If you do not exercise your best judgment, what you bring to the interview can cost you an offer.

> Heather came to a clerkship interview with a prestigious "feeder" judge carrying a large bottle of water. With a look on her face that said "I've got to get through this," she set the bottle on the judge's antique oak desk. Several times during the interview, she took a sip from her bottle and placed it loudly back on the desk. The judge did not give her an offer because he decided he did not want to work with a clerk so lacking in respect and common sense.

You—not your stuff—should be the center of attention at an interview. Leave your drink, coat, and bag elsewhere. There will almost always be a designated storage area you can use. Consider closets, hotel suites, empty classrooms, or receptionists' desks. Use them to store everything except your packet; this way, you will not waste valuable time trying to find a place for your things in the interviewing room. Women who want to carry their handbags to interviews should consider interviewing without them, unless they can find something that looks unobtrusive and professional (thin, dark, medium-sized, and no bright buckles or chains). See Chapter 5 for further discussion on this subject. Of course, cellphones and BlackBerries have no place in the interviewing room.

> Gayle, a senior partner, told us about a candidate who came highly recommended by her colleagues. Gayle was looking forward to the interview because the candidate had strong credentials, and she already contemplated giving him an offer. The candidate, however, showed up to the interview with an iced mocha. He kept slurping the mocha during the interview, with a noise so distracting and unbearable that, at one point, Gayle had to ask him to stop. The mocha made it impossible for this interviewee to receive an offer.

If you must bring anything at all to the interviewing room, it should look professional and not take up too much space. And do not forget to hide any marketing materials you may have just received from other firms. Think of it as bringing a picture of your ex to your first date—just a little awkward! Finally, no matter how tempting it may be, do not place your things on the interviewer's desk or table; according to various studies on nonverbal communication and human behavior, this can translate as an invasion of space.

To sum up, what you bring to the interview paints a picture of how organized you are as a person and as a lawyer. Approaching your interviews in an organized manner can help you make the interviewing process more manageable. What's more, after you prepare a packet of information for one employer, it is fairly easy to duplicate that effort for other interviews. This way, you can maximize your chances with all potential employers while the time and cost of preparation increase only marginally. Remember, an interview is an excellent opportunity to show potential employers that you are on top of things.

QuickReview

✓ Bring a packet of information about yourself, with your resume, transcripts, writing samples, and list of references, to each of your interviews.

✓ After you think you are done proofreading your resume, proof-read it again.

✓ Make sure your resume is on one page, and that your writing sample does not exceed 10 pages.

✓ Contact your references in advance to make sure they are willing to serve as such.

✓ Avoid bringing unnecessary items to the interview.

✓ Anything you bring to the interviewing room should be kept to a minimum and look professional.

Chapter 5

WHAT TO WEAR

You must be well-dressed for your legal interviews if you want to make a good first impression. It is amazing how many intelligent, otherwise qualified candidates lose interview points because they ignore the basic dress code. Some women, for example, make the mistake of wearing short skirts, pantsuits, or tank tops to their interviews. Some men forgo ties, sport garish colors, or wear too much cologne. Even worse, some candidates interview in clothing that is stained or wrinkled. If you want potential employers to take you seriously, do not overlook the importance of dressing for success. If you have any questions about appropriate interviewing attire, ask your career counselors, the firm's recruiting coordinator, or your friends or classmates. You want your interviewers to remember you for your grades, resume, and personality, not your tie, shirt, and shoes.

Dress Conservatively

There is a reason corporate America is labeled as faceless, bland, and boring. For the most part it is, and dress codes reflect that. Law firms, especially big firms that serve as corporate America's lawyers, are even more so. They are conservative workplaces, and they expect their recruits to look the part.

What is deemed as appropriate for interview attire varies somewhat by location. For example, job applicants in the South must wear the most conservative attire. This includes a black, navy, or charcoal gray suit, dark shoes, and a skirt and pantyhose for women. Although you may get away with a brown or light gray suit in the Northeast or the West Coast, dark colors are preferable for all locations. And women, no matter where you are, do not pull a *Legally Blonde* and wear red or pink. A legal interview is not the time to make a fashion statement.

A partner from a prominent Southern law firm may overlook the fact that a female candidate is wearing pants, provided she dazzles him with her credentials and personality. Likewise, he may cut a break to a male candidate who is wearing a light suit if the candidate is truly impressive in all other respects. But in borderline cases, these minor details may break the tie of uncertainty and result in no offer. Accordingly, a traditional dark suit for all of your interviews is advisable.

Wear a Traditional Suit

For women: If you were on the Harvard Law Review, wearing pants to an interview may not hurt your chances; generally, however, a suit with a skirt is preferable. Just make sure that your suit is dark, and that the skirt is a modest length. A skirt that ends slightly above the knee is appropriate; a skirt that is four or more inches above the knee is not. Likewise, do not wear a skirt that is too tight or one with a slit that is too high.

For men: Your suit should be a dark solid color, preferably charcoal gray, navy blue, or black. These colors will match anything, will look professional, and will not indicate a hint of personality. Light gray, brown, olive, or pinstriped suits may be okay, or they may not. The partner interviewing you just might think your striped suit suggests lack of the seriousness and maturity required for the practice of law. Back when he interviewed for an associate position, he had to wear a dark suit—why should that be any different for you? The point is, you just never know. Wearing a traditional dark suit ensures that the major part of your interview ensemble meets the mark.

Even if you already have one acceptable suit in your closet, consider investing in another one. It is always good to have a backup suit, which will also come in handy once you get a job. Barring the rare case of an airline losing your luggage while flying to a callback interview, there is no excuse for not wearing a suit to an interview. We knew one student in law school whose only suit got stuck at the dry cleaners, and who had to show up to his on-campus interviews wearing trousers and a shirt. His appearance was not well-received, and, despite his good grades and charming personality, he was not rewarded with a single callback. (And, no, he did not sue the dry cleaners.)

Your suit should be neither too inexpensive nor too costly. You want to dazzle your interviewers with your personality, not your suit. The associate interviewing you should not be thinking, "Damn, is that punk wearing Armani? Meanwhile the only work experience on his resume is that of a lifeguard? Spoiled brat!" No reason to arouse such animosity and make that associate feel badly about his or her current station in life, mortgage, and student loans, or his or her inability to afford designer clothing. Stick with the less expensive, more popular brands. Think about it this way: If Land's End is good enough for David Boies, it is good enough for you.

Just Say No to Business Casual

Although there are a number of law firms that have adopted business casual as their standard dress code, never assume that you can arrive to an interview this way. Even if you are instructed to dress down for an interview, ignore this advice! Your interviewers already have jobs. You don't.

> Irina recently interviewed at a prestigious firm known for its relaxed working environment and casual dress code. The recruiting coordinator who set up Irina's interview told her to dress casually, emphasizing the fact that the firm management welcomed casual attire, and that most of their candidates wore casual clothes to their interviews. Irina did not comply with these instructions and wore a traditional dark suit to her interview instead. She discovered she made a wise choice. It turned out that the hiring partner who was the key decision-maker in Irina's hiring disapproved of the casual dress code. In fact, this partner always wore suits to the office, even though most of his colleagues dressed casually. Irina firmly believes that she owes her job at this firm to wearing a suit that day.

Many of your interviewers may honestly think that by inviting you to dress casually to an interview, they are advertising one of the firm's biggest perks. Nevertheless, they will subconsciously judge you if you follow their advice and dress down. With the possible exception of very laid-back firms, entertainment companies, and small boutiques, it is almost never appropriate to wear anything other than traditional business attire to a legal interview. But there is also no need to inform the recruiting coordinator about your plan to disregard his or her advice and wear a suit. Simply show up wearing one. No one will ever fault you for dressing in a way that advertises your respect for the position and your professionalism.

Shirts

For men: Your shirt should be neatly pressed and clean, never too expensive (your interviewers may resent you), and in a solid color. Even if you think they accentuate your best features, avoid patterns and stripes—they are simply not formal enough for this occasion. Stick with light colors: white or blue are two most traditional and appropriate colors for interviews. Do not experiment—this is not the time for light pink, lavender, yellow, or light green. Regardless of what is in style, these colors are never appropriate to wear to an interview. Although some candidates may get away with wearing a striped shirt, if someone says, "Hey, cool-looking shirt," then it is probably too much. Wearing a white undershirt to interviews is considered good etiquette, and it will prevent you from sweating through if you become nervous. The best undershirt for this occasion is a cotton crewneck.

Finally, stick with regular cuffs, which look more traditional and less flashy than their French counterparts. If you must wear a shirt with French cuffs, wear it with plain button cufflinks—nothing fancy. Efforts to dazzle your interviewers will almost always backfire. Remember who your audience is. Most of your interviewers are at least 10 to 20 years your senior. When they interviewed for jobs, plain traditional shirts and suits were the only acceptable interview attire. Accordingly, the less you stand out, the better.

For women: The rule is the same as for men. Stick with light, solid colors. If you insist on wearing stripes, choose a shirt with very light stripes. Avoid ruffled or low-cut blouses, which can trigger a negative reaction. If you are interviewing during the summer, consider wearing a short-sleeved shirt to reduce sweating. But keep in mind that although a short-sleeved shirt is an effective way to escape the summer heat, it is still unacceptable to many conservative interviewers. So remember to keep your jacket on at all times. Attorneys in cities such as Orlando, Dallas, and Kansas City will tell you that they do not want to see candidates wearing anything less than a long-sleeved shirt. Ellen, an associate at a regional firm, told us about a summer associate candidate who almost did not get an offer because she wore a short-sleeved shirt to an interview. Although the candidate appeared well-dressed at first, when she took off her jacket at her lunch interview, the interviewers were not at all pleased to discover she was wearing a short-sleeved shirt underneath.

Some women believe that tank tops and T-shirts are entirely appropriate for interviews in warmer climates, and that sweaters are appropriate for cold weather. We advise against this, and here is why: We once overheard a conversation between two judges about a woman who wore a tank top to a clerkship interview. One judge remarked, "She is not fooling anyone. I know that's a tank top she is wearing underneath her jacket. Is she too careless, or is she too lazy to iron her shirt?" Although it is more acceptable for women attorneys to wear T-shirts, tank tops, or sweaters to the office, candidates interviewing for law jobs do not have this luxury. Accordingly, do not follow this trend until you actually have a job. At best, you will look unprofessional; at worst, the interviewer will assume that you do not care enough about the position because you did not bother to dress appropriately.

Ties

Our friend Hugh thought he might make an impression by wearing a blindingly pink tie to an on-campus interview (in his defense, it was Thomas Pink, and he made it look good). The first thing one of the interviewers said to him was, "Wow, that's a ballsy tie." That is how pink it was. We do not know if this tie had any effect on the number of callbacks Hugh received, but we can say the following with some certainty: the tie should have some color, but it should not be your distinguishing feature. The interviewers' attention should be drawn to you, not your attire, and certainly not your tie. In fact, a number of interviewers commented negatively on this behavior, pointing out that garish colors are never appropriate for an interview. Although unusual colors may get the interviewer's attention, it may not be the attention you want.

You may notice some of your interviewers are sporting snazzy ties. We recall one on-campus interviewer wearing a beautiful Hermès tie (despite his lack of seniority). All the female law students talked about the tie, which made his employer, a well-known Chicago-based firm, seem quite stylish. The interviewer and his firm were a hit that day. But as an interviewee, you should not mimic your interviewers' appearance. Keep in mind that, regardless of their age and position at the firm, it is their opportunity to look important and to get some attention from admiring law students. You, on the other hand, need a job, not attention. So stick with Banana Republic for now.

Of course, there is something to be said for attire that inspires confidence, yours and the interviewer's. In your efforts to dress conservatively and professionally, do not be afraid to wear that favorite tie that makes you look and feel confident. Overly flamboyant dress, however, may have the opposite effect, signaling to interviewers that you are not confident in your ability to stand out and make an impression. Your interviewers are looking for the candidate who stands out on his own accord, not the one who needs a fuchsia tie to be memorable. Ultimately, your confidence in your ability to get the job is just as important as showing that you know how to play the interviewing game.

As a general rule, do not wear a striped tie if you are wearing a striped suit or a striped shirt (which are not recommended for an interview anyway). It is best to wear a solid tie to compliment the stripes. Additionally, although there is a wide range of acceptable colors, stick with conservative colors and stay away from unusual patterns. Do not wear a black tie or a tie that doesn't match the rest of your attire. If you are wearing a black suit, make sure that either your tie or your shirt is a lighter color to avoid looking as though you just came from a wedding or a funeral. Here is a helpful tidbit of information regarding psychological effects of colors on the audience: During presidential debates, male candidates typically wear either a solid red or blue tie. This is because red communicates leadership and control, and blue projects calmness, composure, and organization. No matter what color you choose, however, show your interviewers that you can tie a handsome knot.

Finally, carry a handkerchief with you so that you can wipe off your hands shortly before an interview if they become sweaty. But do not place it in the outside breast pocket of your jacket—it will make you look like a gangster, not a job candidate.

Shoes and Accessories

For men: This is the easy part. Classic, lace-up black leather shoes shined to perfection will do the trick. Brown shoes are acceptable, but black is a safer color. Make sure your shoes are clean and that they match your belt. These items, along with your watch, are statistically the top items that will be noticed by your female interviewers (and which will likely be ignored by their male counterparts). Stick with an unobtrusive, preferably silver-toned, belt buckle. If you decide to wear a watch, make sure it is not too expensive, and try to pick one that matches your belt buckle and has a leather band. As a rule of thumb, your socks should be the same color as or darker than your suit. Avoid patterned socks, and never wear white or light-colored socks. Make sure your socks are over-the-calf—you do not want to show skin when you cross your legs during an interview.

For women: Although our advice is, once again, to be conservative, you actually have many choices when it comes to shoes. The main point to remember here is that your shoes should be black, with covered toes and back. The rest is up to you—the designer, the style, and the heel height do not matter, as long as you do not go overboard. You want your shoes to look professional, not escort-service professional.

> This is the mistake Amberly made during her interview at a major East Coast firm. She wore a dark skirt suit, stockings, minimal jewelry, and black lace-up shoes. To her credit, the shoes were close toed, and the rest of her wardrobe looked very conservative. However, the partner who interviewed her later remarked that there was absolutely no way she would consider giving an offer to someone wearing "ballet slippers." There was no offer, despite the fact that Amberly had excellent credentials and was about to graduate from a top-tier school.

Women are more likely to be judged unfairly at an interview because of how they dress. Moreover, there are more pitfalls out there for female candidates than there are for their male counterparts in terms of dress code. As a result, women should be extra attentive to their interviewing attire.

In most Southern states, women still wear skirts and pantyhose to an interview. In other parts of the country, pantsuits or skirts without stockings are becoming the norm. When in doubt, wear a skirt and pantyhose if weather permits. This is especially true if your skin is pale, which would make the fact that you are not wearing pantyhose more noticeable. Pick a neutral, solid color (black pantyhose have only been recently adopted by the business world and should be worn with caution), and be prepared for unpleasant little surprises.

> Kim, an associate interviewing to make a lateral move, was walking into her first interview when she discovered a huge hole in her stockings. Fortunately, she was able to calmly proceed to the bathroom, pull out a spare pair of stockings from her purse, change, and be back in time for her interview.

Handbags and briefcases

With regard to handbags and briefcases, our advice is to leave them behind. They do not serve any function at an interview. The only thing you really need and should bring into the interviewing room is a folder/portfolio with your marketing materials (resume, writing samples, transcripts, and so on). You can even hide things such as car keys or a credit card in this folder, in case you must carry them with you.

Handbags and briefcases can be distracting for you and your interviewers. They look bulky when you carry them around, you must figure out where to put them without invading the interviewer's personal space, and they can open and reveal their contents. Furthermore, it is difficult to pick the right interview bag—especially a handbag. Most handbags are too flashy and trendy, and some can make you look unprofessional. Therefore, try to leave your briefcase or bag at home or in the car, or ask the receptionist or a recruiting coordinator to store it for you. If you must bring it to an interview, choose a small black purse with no flashy buckles or accessories (for women), or a thin black or brown briefcase (for men). It should close easily, be simply designed, and not draw unnecessary attention to itself. Once you are in the interviewing room, remember not to place your bag on the desk or table so as not to invade the interviewer's space. Instead, place it on a chair next to you or under your seat.

Hair and grooming

For men: No matter how well you are dressed, long or untidy hair will create a disconnect between you and your professional attire. That said, avoid a $500 John Edwards special or spiked hair—both can antagonize your interviewers. Supercuts will probably do, as all you are aiming for is clean-cut and professional. Trim your eyebrows, make sure your hair is neat and clean around the neckline and ears, with trimmed sideburns. If you have time and money, invest in teeth-whitening strips.

For women: Your hair should look professional and elegant. If your hair is long, you can tie it in a ponytail, wear a thin, solid, dark-colored headband, pin your hair up, or style it in some other conservative way. Just do not go for the Barbie look and let all of your hair down; your interviewer may not take you seriously, especially if you are a blonde. Short hair should be neat and styled. Try not to make any drastic changes to your hair shortly before the interviews, and consider whitening your teeth. Stained teeth, a bad haircut, and uneven highlights can all diminish your confidence.

Fragrance and makeup

For men: Always use a deodorant, but avoid colognes and aftershaves that emit a strong scent. Nobody wants to hire an attorney who will be nicknamed "too-much-cologne guy." Some interviewers suggest forgoing cologne entirely to avoid such issues as allergies.

For women: You have a wide range of fragrance choices available to you, and it is fine to wear a light fragrance to the interview. Some studies suggest that women are more confident when wearing perfume and makeup, and that employers prefer women who wear perfume to those who do not. The most important advice here is not to overdo it. Be considerate of your interviewers. Makeup and perfume should be noticeable, but they should not call unnecessary attention to themselves. We have all had to ride in an elevator at some point with a gal who went perfume crazy—not a pleasant experience. Stick to light scents. Excessive makeup is likely to raise a red flag with potential employers, as well. Choose neutral eye shadows, subtle blush, and light foundation if your skin permits it. Shy away from very dark or very bright lipsticks. You are not interviewing for a Broadway show.

Jewelry, tattoos, and piercings

Candidates interviewing in New York can generally get away with more than interviewees in, say, Atlanta. But generally, unless you are interviewing for a position with an up-and-coming entertainment company, the interviewers are not going to appreciate your sense of style and uniqueness when it comes to tattoos and piercings. Visible tattoos should be covered with makeup, and piercings should be removed. According to one partner, although making hiring decisions is always difficult because there is such a large pool of qualified applicants, some candidates make it too easy: "One candidate came to an interview with his tongue pierced," he said. "I liked him, but how could I present him to the hiring committee?" The next logical question might as well have been, "How could I present him to a client?"

Virtually all employers have a predictable preference when it comes to jewelry—the less the better. Therefore, no matter where you are interviewing, go easy on the jewelry. There are only four pieces of jewelry a woman should wear to an interview: earrings, a ring, a simple necklace, and a watch. For men, the only acceptable jewelry is a watch and a wedding band or a class ring. Never wear lapel pins to an interview; whether it is a patriotic flag pin or a yellow ribbon, making a political statement at an interview is simply not appropriate. When it comes to rings, it is best if the only ring on the candidate's finger is a wedding ring (if he or she is married). Earrings (one in each ear!) are appropriate for women only, and they should not be long or flashy. Finally, women can wear either a strand of pearls or a delicate necklace, as long as it does not cry for attention.

> Sarah, a first-year law student, wore a Swarovski crystal pendent to an interview. The entire time, an older partner was staring at her chest, making her wonder if he was about to sexually harass her. She felt uncomfortable during the interview, only to find out later that the partner thought she was sporting a 3-carat diamond! At the end of the interview, the partner asked her about the stone, suggesting that she didn't need a legal job if she could afford such fancy jewelry.

The moral of this story is do not invite unnecessary attention.

As you can see, all these conservative suggestions paint a picture of a professional lawyer in very boring colors of black and charcoal gray, not leaving much possibility for excitement or style. Unfortunately, this is how lawyers are expected to look. Whether at a corporate law firm or in a government office, attorneys are not expected to distinguish themselves by their appearance. This is especially true in private practice, where law firms see themselves as an extension of the corporate clients they serve. By dressing conservatively, you demonstrate that you know how things work in the legal world, which will make your interviewers that much more predisposed to your candidacy.

QuickReview

✓ Geography matters. Consider whether your outfit is region appropriate.

✓ Always wear a suit, even if told not to by your recruiter or interviewer.

✓ Dress conservatively; do not wear anything flashy or too expensive.

✓ Stick with solid colors: white and light blue for shirts; red, blue, or other traditional colors for ties; navy, charcoal gray, or black for suits; and black for shoes.

✓ Do not wear a tank top, T-shirt, or sweater to your interviews.

✓ If you wear a short-sleeved shirt, remember to keep your jacket on at all times.

✓ The only acceptable jewelry includes a watch and a wedding ring (for men and women), and earrings and a simple necklace (for women).

✓ Men should wear socks that are the same color as or darker than their shoes; women should opt for beige pantyhose.

✓ If you have questions about appropriate attire, ask your career services, friends and family, or the firm's recruiting coordinator.

✓ Be memorable because of who you are, not what you wear.

Chapter 6

How to Sell Yourself Effectively

Regardless of your credentials and experience, once you get the interview, you must put your best foot forward. True, some firms have strict GPA cutoffs; and even if you are an interviewing rock star, these Wachtells and Cravaths will not give you the light of day if you do not meet their criteria. But the good news is, for the vast majority of legal employers, these criteria are not set in stone. So when you are sitting across the table from your interviewers, you can convince them to hire you despite any preconceived notions they may have about you after seeing your resume. Here is how.

Emphasize Your Strong Points

An advocate by calling, you must learn early in your career to use your strong points to your advantage. Employers seek out candidates who are confident in their abilities and can articulate their strengths. They are reluctant to hire candidates who are insecure or unable to sell themselves during an interview. The reason for this is simple: Legal employers do not want to hire unskilled advocates or those who will need motivation and/or reassurance to get the job done.

When Tanya interviewed as a lateral associate, she was uncertain about her strengths and lacked confidence in her skills. Identifying what made her a good attorney provided her with good sales-pitch material for her interview. Tanya began analyzing her skills by reviewing her old memos and billing records to determine what areas she aced and where she needed improvement. She also asked her mentors and senior colleagues for feedback about her performance. She discovered they strongly valued her research skills because she could find answers to the most obscure questions. She also noted her

> history of writing winning motions. This helped her gain the confidence she needed to ace her interview and score major points by being one of the few candidates who gave concrete examples of strengths, rather than just naming them.

Analyze your strengths and prepare a sales pitch in advance of your interview. And if you do not yet know what your strengths are, figure it out by evaluating your law school performance, completed projects, and feedback from mentors and colleagues. If you are fresh from law school, for example, your good grades may indicate you are hardworking. Or, if your GPA is nothing to write home about, you can use high grades on certain subjects to explain how the employer will benefit from your expertise in that area of law. Similarly, you can note that the firm's corporate department can utilize your business skills. You can even emphasize your leadership positions and memberships in organizations as a sign of hard work, people skills, and commitment.

Once you know your strengths, prioritize them as you were taught to do in legal writing and make your strongest points first. Due to time constraints, you may never have a chance to address them all. Do not recite a long list of strengths, or you may risk boring your interviewer. Think about your strengths ahead of time so that they can roll off your tongue with the ease of "negligent infliction of emotional distress." This way, you will sound prepared and convincing. But make sure you pause before you speak. Employers are more impressed with the candidates who think on their feet than with those who memorize their answers. If you are not asked about your strengths directly, build a discussion about them into your conversation. Regardless of what direction the conversation turns, you must find a way to explain why you are the one candidate this employer needs.

Address Your Weak Points

A good interview is an exercise of confidence. Do not be insecure, and do not try to preempt questions by admitting your faults or weak points on your resume. Do not start any statements with "I'm not the best at academics, but...." Always discuss your strengths, but never bring up any weaknesses unless you are specifically asked about them.

Which brings us to the next question: What if they ask? Some interviewers like to ask you to name your strengths and weaknesses. Have your list of strengths memorized. With respect to the weaknesses, never say that you do not know of any or that you do not have any—you will only sound clueless or arrogant. The truth is, your weaknesses matter less than your ability to understand and improve them.

If you are asked, always give an example of one weak point, but never discuss work-related mistakes. Furthermore, always emphasize that you do not have any weaknesses that would interfere with your ability to do your job. It is a good idea to talk about mistakes that happened in the past, that you corrected and learned from, or simply ones that are not relevant to your work. For example, you can say that you found learning a foreign language challenging, that you are a poor test-taker, that you had to learn not to micromanage, or that you used to have difficulties working on a team. Always follow up with an explanation of how you tackled this weakness and a subsequent discussion of your strengths.

Finally, do not give examples of weaknesses that are really strengths. Employers see this as a disingenuous attempt to avoid answering the question. Here are some examples: "I am a perfectionist—I do not let go of a project until I am completely satisfied," "I do not delegate very well, and thus I tend to put a great deal of effort into my projects," and "Sometimes I micromanage by following through on an entire project."

Answer the "Why" Question

Very often, an interviewer may ask why you want to work at a particular firm or organization or why he or she should hire you. Occasionally, this question comes in a more subtle form.

> One hiring partner revealed to us that he asks every interviewee, from the most junior summer associate candidate to a senior lateral partner, two questions. The first one is, "Imagine we hired you. Several months later, at a cocktail party, I ask your colleagues what they think about working with you. What would they say?" His follow-up question is, "Now, imagine, at the same party, I ask you what you think about the firm so far." This partner is not looking for any particular response. But a one-sided, rehearsed, cookie-cutter answer about how great you and the firm are may disqualify you. What he wants is a genuine answer that gives two sides of the story. After discussing your strengths, what do your colleagues think you could do better? After mentioning the things you really like (hope to like) about this firm, do you have any suggestions for improvement?

To every interviewer, "why" is the most important question. Your answer must demonstrate thoughtfulness, confidence, your good fit within the firm, and your genuine desire to work there. This is not the time to retreat, give a disingenuous response, or rest on a short, one-sentence answer. This is the time to sell yourself by explaining that you are a hard worker, and that your particular skills make you ideal for the job. Because your answer must be well-researched and sufficiently detailed, preparation is key.

Distinguish Yourself

Most of the interviewees in our field share a similar profile. They are young; they went to law school straight out of college; they have little or no work experience; they have good grades from a good school, or stellar grades from a lower-ranked school; or they have experience that makes them a good candidate. There is nothing truly unique about this package, and these qualities alone rarely impress interviewers or make a candidate stand out. Therefore, you must take every interview as an opportunity to distinguish yourself from the rest of the crowd in some way, whether it is by your level of preparation, your witty charm, or your strong communication skills. If you approach every interview as the most important 20 minutes in your life, your efforts, time, and preparation will help you succeed.

What you must remember is that there was something about you that got you this interview in the first place. All you need to do now is go beyond that "something" and show the interviewer that there is more to you than your resume. Interviewers see so many qualified candidates that sometimes it becomes difficult to tell them apart. This is why who you are matters—you have an opportunity to be remembered as someone interesting, unique, or outstanding. Focus on your strengths rather than your weaknesses, and give the interviewer every single reason you can think of for him or her to hire you.

QuickReview

✓ Sell yourself to the interviewer by demonstrating the unique qualities that distinguish you from the pool of interviewees.

✓ Approach every interview with the utmost confidence in your ability to get the job.

✓ Remember that there is usually a good reason why you received an interview in the first place.

✓ Emphasize your strengths during the interview, starting with your strongest points.

✓ Your ability to discuss your strong points during an interview signals to the employer that you can get the job done without handholding.

✓ Do not talk about your weaknesses unless you are asked to, and never dwell on them.

✓ Do not discuss prior mistakes, or employers may think of you as a liability.

Chapter 7

BODY LANGUAGE AND DEMEANOR

Interviewing is like dating: It involves the art of mutual seduction and possible commitment. You are trying to look attractive to potential employers, while they are trying to woo you in turn. You use interviews to figure out if you are a good match. After an employer is willing to commit, you may tell them you are not ready to settle down until you see what else is out there. In this delicate interviewing dance, body language and demeanor are some of your strongest weapons—assuming you use them correctly.

Find the Right Balance of Confidence

Although it is important to exhibit confidence during an interview, make sure your confidence is not read as arrogance. No matter how much interest you are receiving from legal employers, you still need to work hard to receive offers. A cocky demeanor and arrogant questions can alienate potential employers.

> According to one recruiting coordinator, her firm screens out arrogant candidates, no matter how superb their credentials are. She recalled a story about a candidate with such an extreme sense of entitlement that he asked, "Your firm is not ranked in the Vault top 10. Why should I consider working for you?" His interviewer was so turned off by this remark that he reported it to the law school career services and advised the firm against hiring the candidate, despite his strong credentials.

On the flip side, do not exhibit a complete lack of confidence. Some interviewees are so insecure that they spend valuable interview time practically begging for an offer and pointing out their own weaknesses.

Dan's interviewers were friendly and tried to make him feel at ease during his lateral interview. Encouraged by their positive attitude, Dan let his guard down and made his insecurities known. He told them he did not get offers from the three other firms where he interviewed. He then complained about his grim prospects at his current firm. Uncomfortable with the situation, one of the interviewers tried to console Dan. Dan's reply was, "You can make it right. Give me a job. Please!" Needless to say, an offer was not in the cards.

Find the right balance of confidence. Believing in yourself can help interviewers believe in you. But being needy, insecure, cocky, or arrogant cannot inspire an offer. Exhibit the right level of confidence by being courteous, polite, and pleasant; by being a good listener; by asking follow-up questions; and by being involved in the conversation without dominating it.

Try Not to Be Nervous

Unless you have a great deal of experience, you are probably going to be nervous. Even seasoned interviewees occasionally get butterflies. Being nervous weighs you down, makes the interview seem endless, and makes you look uptight. More importantly, it prevents you from being who you are—a bright lawyer with personality and charm. Although being nervous is not something you can easily control, you can learn to mask it.

Remember that practice makes perfect. The best preparation for an interview—aside from reading this book, of course—is to sit down for a mock interview. Pretend it is the real deal: have your "interviewer" ask you questions, practice your answers, do not crack jokes, and replay less-than-perfect answers until you get them right. This preparation will be invaluable when you are at the real interview. You will stop worrying and start thinking, and you will instantly know how to answer even the most difficult questions.

Make a conscious effort not to be nervous. We will stop short of asking you to picture your interviewers naked, as we are not sure this advice actually works. But do use the techniques that work for you. Whether it is praying, working out, being thoroughly prepared, or reminding yourself to relax, find what helps you be less nervous. Studies show that physical exercise helps reduce nervousness, which can improve your interview performance. This is because the exercise helps reduce the level of adrenaline in the body. So take the stairs or walk to the interview.

Engage Your Interviewer

Some career counselors may instruct you to focus solely on your skills and credentials during your interviews. The reasoning behind this advice is that you only have a short time to demonstrate you are qualified, and you will not receive an offer if you waste precious time on small talk. Having been on both sides of the interviewing table, we can confidently tell you this is the worst advice you can get.

Some of the best interviews that result in prompt offers have nothing to do with the law or credentials. They involve discussions about cooking, halibut fishing, or traveling across Europe. The reason? These conversations are much more interesting and engaging than discussions about the law, and they help the interviewer relate to the candidate.

> Mary is a mid-level associate at a prominent New Orleans firm. Every year, Mary's firm hires 10 summer associates, but at the end of the summer only a few receive offers. According to Mary, the firm uses informal interviews to decide who gets an offer. These interviews are so informal, in fact, that the summer associates do not even realize they are being interviewed. The firm's technique is simple: At the end of the summer, each associate is taken out for a nice, long lunch by his or her mentor. The mentor then prepares a formal evaluation about their conversation, the student's demeanor, and, most importantly, whether the student was fun to be around. In the last two years, the only summer associates who received offers (after producing quality work, of course) were those who managed to make these lunches personal and fun for the interviewer. Most of these candidates did not talk about the law at all.

Tell a Story

You can give the best, the most correct, and the most prepared answers to the interviewer's questions. But you will still sound bland and boring if you do not inject personality into your answers.

> During her clerkship interview, Karen impressed the judge with her professional attire, her confident demeanor, and her resume. Sadly, Karen lacked the ability to tell a coherent story. Every time the judge asked her a question, Karen found a way to give short answers, often stopping with a yes or no, and sometimes even using inappropriate informal tone by answering with a "yeah." Despite Karen's stellar credentials, the judge did not extend her an offer because Karen's short and unprofessional answers made it difficult for the judge to relate to her on a personal level.

Be a storyteller during your interviews, and your interviewers will listen with great interest. If you can, accompany certain answers with examples. For example, if your interviewer asks you about your clerkship, tell him or her how your judge loved to put his feet up while talking to you about the law, and how much you had learned on those occasions. If your interviewer asks you about your previous job experience, mention the time you received a call from a very important client and had to handle an urgent matter by yourself while the partner was out of reach. The stories you tell will convey a much better picture of what you have learned, who you are, and why you should get the job. They will engage your interviewer in a way straightforward answers cannot.

Engage in Flattery

Another important trick of the interviewing trade is flattery. Whether you are interviewing as a senior lateral attorney or a 1L, you will be surprised how far flattery can get you, and how receptive the interviewers are to compliments. The trick is to be prepared and to sound so genuine that the interviewer does not see through you. If you think about it, this is pretty easy. With tools such as Google, Martindale-Hubble, and attorney profiles on firm Websites, there is plenty of information out there that you can use to butter up the decision-makers. Plus, no one loves themselves more than lawyers, and no one loves to talk about themselves more than lawyers. Just look at those attorney profiles. Guess who writes them? The attorneys themselves. So if your interviewer chooses to put his or her marathon training or book-writing experience in his or her bio, by all means talk about it.

Chapter 3 discusses what you can do to prepare for an interview. After reviewing it, find a few interesting facts about your interviewer (or facts you can pretend are interesting). This will help you engage with the interviewer over something he or she knows and can talk about, and make you seem genuinely interested in his or her achievements. All in all, unless you discovered the name of your interviewer minutes before an interview, a failure to prepare will not be excused.

Cassidy recently made a lateral move to another firm. While she was preparing for her interview, she discovered that there were only two partners among her interviewers, and they would undoubtedly have a great deal of say in whether to hire her. Cassidy, who was interested in this firm because of its product liability practice, discovered that the first partner actually practiced healthcare law, and the second was a patent litigator. Cassidy knew nothing about these areas, so she spent a great deal of time researching them. To her amazement, she really liked learning about healthcare law. In fact, after a very

> pleasant meeting with the first partner, Cassidy joined the firm
> and now practices in that area. Her meeting with the IP partner
> went just as well. Even though she did not know much about his
> practice area, she was able to show genuine interest in it. Both
> times, she used flattery by telling the partners how little she knew
> about their practice before the interview, and how interested
> she became in it after reading their works, reviewing their cases,
> and talking to them.

There is, of course, a thin line between flattering and openly flirting with your interviewer. Hopefully you know where this line is, and you must never cross it. Pleasant and genuine flattery can help you turn a boring interview into a fascinating conversation, and secure an offer where you otherwise would not receive it. But it can backfire if you do not do it right, so proceed with caution.

Body Language

First impressions matter. Your handshake should be neither too weak nor too strong, and you should sit up straight but appear relaxed. Do not slouch or sit on the edge of your chair. Place your arms where your interviewer can see them, with your palms open (this shows that you have nothing to hide). Maintain good eye contact at all times. Do not use too many gestures because they may distract your interviewer. Lean forward a little bit to show interest, but do not lean so much that you invade the interviewer's personal space or seem too eager.

If you want to be convincing, remember to speak in a firm voice and to pause in order to emphasize your next point. Slow down, or the interviewer may not understand you. If you are asked a difficult question, always pause before answering, even if you know the answer. This will help you sound genuine. You can also look up before answering difficult questions. People look up when they try to re-create an answer from a mental picture in their head. Some studies suggest that looking away from the interviewer before answering a difficult question can help you concentrate. Just do not look to your left, because it is a nonverbal cue that you are about to lie.

Finally, be friendly and conversational, and, above all, genuine. Remember to smile, even if the interviewer does not. By all means, laugh at his or her jokes, regardless of how unfunny they are. Finally, if you are having difficulty relating to the interviewer, imagine that he or she is someone you care deeply about, such as a beloved aunt or uncle. Every time you answer a question, remind yourself that you really like this person. Not only will this help you relax, but it will also help you exhibit interest and attentiveness.

Your demeanor should be the nonverbal counterpart of your message to your future employer—"I am qualified, smart, confident, and you will enjoy working with me." Your interviewers have already seen your resume and have gauged your qualifications and experience. Now they are curious to actually see the person behind the resume. Show them the best of who you are and engage them in conversation. At the end of your interview, the interviewer should feel that you sincerely appreciated his or her time and efforts, and that the interview was a pleasant break from the busy workday.

QuickReview

✓ Focus on your strengths and exhibit confidence, but do not act like you already have an offer.

✓ Do not let your insecurities or nervousness show.

✓ Engage your interviewer by listening carefully, asking follow-up questions, and telling a story with your answers.

✓ Spend at least a part of your interview on subjects outside the law to help engage your interviewer.

✓ Use flattery, but do not cross the fine line between flattery and harassment.

✓ Be mindful of your body language and demeanor; sit up straight, place your hands where the interviewer can see them, smile, and do not use too many gestures.

✓ Remember to pause and speak slowly.

Part II

❦

Tackling the Questions

Chapter 8

QUESTIONS TO ASK

Almost every interview culminates with the dreaded question, "Do you have any questions?" You may be so happy to have survived the interview that asking questions is the last thing you want to do. But if you feel the urge to blurt out that you have no questions, stop and think: "No" is the wrong answer here! Asking questions is an important part of the interviewing game. Questions communicate your ability to initiate and engage in a conversation. Additionally, they help you learn about the firm. Meanwhile, a lack of questions gives out an impression that you are not serious about the job.

Correct Answer #1: "I Have Several Questions"

Ideally, you will have a few. Just do not say that you have tons, or interviewers will instantly assume that you are either unprepared, that you cannot prioritize your questions, or that it is going to be a very long interview. For some lucky interviewees, asking questions comes naturally. These are usually the candidates who, as law students, managed to answer when called on by a professor and to ask intelligent questions in class, even when they did not do the reading. If you are one of those people, you can probably wing it; if not, prepare your questions in advance. Keep in mind that lawyers appreciate brevity, so keep your questions concise.

Correct Answer #2: "No, Because I Did My Homework"

If you are genuinely prepared and really do not have any questions, or if you are simply too tired to ask them, this answer is the next best thing. (Just be sure to phrase it in an intelligent way and present it with utmost confidence.) Try this: "Well, I have done a great deal of research before coming to this interview. I know a great deal about the firm, and my research convinced me that your firm is the place where I want to be. So, I really do not have any questions. But do you have any additional questions for me?"

Although interviewers look for good, well-thought-out questions about the firm or their own experience, they are usually very pleased to hear that the interviewee did a great deal of research before the interview. Therefore, this answer usually satisfies them almost as much as good, intelligent questions. Don't worry—they are not going to quiz you, trivia style, about the firm to determine if you are telling the truth. However, use this answer only if you must. Ideally, you should always have several questions prepared.

Correct Answer #3: "No, Because You Already Answered Them"

If your interview has indeed been informative, feel free to tell your interviewer that he or she answered all your questions. However, only say this if this is true—if all the interviewer did was grill you for 18 minutes about your credentials, this answer will come off as a disingenuous attempt to avoid asking questions. That said, many of the attorneys we interviewed for this book suggested this as a great answer. So, by popular demand, here it is: "I may have some questions at a later time, but I do not have any questions now. You told me so much about the firm that you already answered all of my questions. After our conversation, I am convinced that your firm is a great place to work." This spoonful of flattery, along with a tad bit of thoughtfulness, may be just enough to secure an offer!

Ask About the Firm

When asking about the firm, you should ask questions that the interviewer can answer easily. Be careful not to make your interviewer feel uncomfortable or unprepared by asking a question that is too narrow or specific. This can lead to an awkward situation, and may end up being the only thing the interviewer remembers about you.

> Emily, a junior associate at a large firm, once had an interviewee ask her about a high-profile case the firm handled. It was a good question, one that showed that the student did his research. The problem was that the case was handled by more senior attorneys, at a different department and from a different office. Emily had to acknowledge that the only thing she knew about the case was what she had heard in the media. She gave the student a lower score on his evaluation because she did not feel this was a "smart question."

In addition, always consider how likely it is that your interviewer will know the answer to your question.

> As a junior associate, Rick interviewed a number of summer associates and lateral candidates who asked him about the partner-selection process, partner compensation, and even about the size of the book of business needed to make partner. The obvious flaw in all of those questions was that they would not be relevant for these candidates for another 10 years or so. The other problem was that Rick had absolutely no idea what the answers were. Rick told the candidates to direct those questions to the partners, hoping they would have enough common sense at least to wait until getting an offer to ask them.

Well-thought-out questions about a firm include inquiries into the work at a particular department, the atmosphere of the office, the firm's pro bono projects, and any other questions that indicate in-depth research. You will get bonus points for starting your questions with, "I noticed that your firm has/does/offers...." Notably, although it is fine to ask about pro bono work, always try to refer to a particular case or project the firm handled. Otherwise, you are entering the "what not to ask" zone, risking leaving your interviewer with an impression that you are more interested in pro bono than billable work.

> Jeremy once interviewed a third-year law student who attended a good law school but whose GPA was somewhat below the firm's recommended cut-off. Nevertheless, she received an offer from the firm because she impressed Jeremy by asking about the firm's signature pro bono project and inquiring whether summer associates could get involved. This project—the firm's pride and joy—was not yet widely publicized, so Jeremy was flattered that she found out about it on her own and then showed initiative by suggesting she wanted to work on it. This was enough to move her above the no-offer margin.

Ask About the Interviewer

No one loves flattery more than lawyers. If you are unable to work flattery into at least one of your questions, you are doing something wrong. This is where our dating analogy is most accurate. Just as you do on a first or second date, you need to connect and develop rapport with your interviewers. The only way to do this is by asking questions about them and searching for things you have in common, thus cultivating fertile ground for a nice, "feel-good" conversation.

You will score major brownie points with the interviewer if you ask him about his experience, achievements, and successes. (And yes, at the risk of sounding male-centric, we say "him" because we believe that women attorneys are more likely to see through you if you use flattery less carefully.) Do not ask overly personal questions—unless you are sitting in the interviewer's office and you want to ask about a photo or a certain collectable on his or her desk.

> One senior partner once made an offer to an associate after he asked the partner about a model of an airplane on his desk. As it turned out, the partner used to be a pilot in the military, and the little plastic plane on his desk was actually a model of the plane he now owned. Imagine the fascinating conversation that followed this question!

Even without tiny airplanes to rescue you, there are plenty of good questions at your disposal. Just look at the interviewers' bios, read their attorney profiles, and, most importantly, listen. Did they go to the same school you did? Did they argue landmark cases? What do they like about their job? Did they previously live in an area familiar to you? Did they study abroad or work in a different country? Knowing their dossier helps you discuss subjects that are familiar to them.

You can also ask about their experience practicing in a certain area. One line of questioning that never fails is to ask how they developed their expertise in this area, what prompted them to pick this specialty, and what advice they have for you with regard to doing the same. Similarly, you can ask general questions about their tenure at the firm. Did they work somewhere else first? What do they like more about their current firm?

If your interviewers frequently speak at conferences, teach, or publish, by all means ask them about these things! Nothing makes attorneys more proud than achieving these milestones. Likewise, if they list the big cases they have won on their bio, they may be eager to talk about them.

> A well-known partner who practices products liability exemplifies this principle. Early in his career, he argued a products liability case before the U.S. Supreme Court. He openly says this was the proudest moment in his life, and he does not get tired of talking about it even 20 years later. Not surprisingly, interviewees who do their homework and know to ask him about the case are very well-received.

The truth is, no matter what you ask, as long as you do not sound like a stalker and do not ask overly personal questions, getting your interviewer to talk will work in your favor. Candidates who engage their interviewers to the point that the interviewers talk more during the interview are more likely to receive offers.

Sample Questions

You should prepare your questions in advance, based on thorough research. However, if research fails you, or if you are pressed for time, or if your interviewer's name changes unexpectedly, here are some good questions you can ask:

✓ How did you grow into this practice area? (For senior associates and partners.)

✓ How did you develop your expertise? (For partners.)

✓ What has your experience been as a junior lawyer at X department?

✓ How is your relationship with your colleagues?

✓ What were the most important things you learned in the first few years of practice?

✓ What would your advice be to someone going into your practice area? (For senior associates and partners.)

✓ Do you encourage junior associates to contribute to the firm's growth, marketing, and client development? (For small firms.)

✓ Do you give junior lawyers a great deal of responsibility early on? (For small firms.)

✓ Can you tell me more about your practice area and the type of clients you serve? (For partners.)

✓ What types of cases and assignments do you get to work on? (For associates.)

✓ If you like a particular type of work, are you able to work on those matters by politely asking? (For junior associates.)

✓ What classes should I take to be more prepared for work at an X department? (If you are a law student.)

✓ Your firm is known for a personal atmosphere in the office and a high level of responsibility for junior associates—can you tell me more about that?

✓ Can you describe the work environment?

✓ What are you looking for in a candidate? (For senior associates and partners.)

✓ What has been your experience in terms of interaction with other offices? (For larger firms.)

✓ Do you think I can use [a particular skill] when working in X department? (Yes, this is a shameless plug incorporated into a question, but it works! Just make sure you ask about a relevant skill.)

✓ Can you tell me more about the training opportunities at your firm? (For larger firms.)

✓ Does the firm have a mentoring program?

This may seem obvious to state, but after you ask a question, actually listen to the answer. You would be surprised how many times interviewees ask a question only to look away or seem uninterested in the response. If you do this, this is a clear indicator that you could not come up with a genuine question, and that you are wasting the interviewer's time. Asking smart follow-up questions reveals that you can listen well and know how to gracefully carry on a conversation.

Finally, if you feel the urge to comment on or compliment the interviewer on his or her answer, do so carefully. For example, you can say, "Thank you so much for taking the time to answer my question. Your answer helped me decide this is the place where I want to work," or "Your answer helped me figure out this difficult issue." Just do not do what one interviewee did. Upon receiving an answer to a difficult question, she commented, "Good answer." The interviewer was flabbergasted by this familiarity. The interviewer could not help but wonder if the candidate realized that *she* was the one being interviewed.

In addition to information they glean, the questions you ask also tell the interviewer something about you. Have you done your homework? Do you have realistic expectations about this job? Were you paying attention to what your interviewer was saying? In many ways, your questions reflect on and help to summarize your interview. Think of them as a logical conclusion to your interaction with the interviewer. If you received plenty of information, just say so. If you have a legitimate question or two, ask them, time permitting. If you feel that you need to ask a question or two just to be polite, perhaps you can follow up on something the interviewer mentioned previously. Ultimately, your questions should show your interest in the firm and your ability to pay attention. If you can do that, an offer may be just a phone call away.

QuickReview

✓ Do your homework and be prepared to ask a few questions going into your interview.

✓ Ask questions that demonstrate your preparation and research; do not ask obvious questions or solicit information you should already know.

✓ Make sure that the interviewer is in a position to answer your questions.

✓ Ask questions that have a predictably positive and flattering answer.

✓ Ask the interviewer questions that will allow him or her to discuss personal milestones, achievements, and successes.
✓ Try to connect with your interviewer on a human level and find common ground between you.

Chapter 9

WHAT NOT TO ASK

A law job interview is very similar to a first date. You must make a good first impression if you want to receive a follow-up invitation. You already have what it takes to get your foot in the door—you would not get an interview if you did not. Now you must also show your interviewer that you are sociable, likeable, and normal. As with first dates, your conversation with potential employers should be pleasant and lighthearted. Just as you would not want to ask about your blind date's income, age, or weight, you do not want to ask intrusive questions at your first interview. The key to a successful interview is to stay away from intrusive topics and avoid the questions discussed in this chapter.

"How much will I make?"

Do not ask questions about salary, partners' incomes, or bonuses. These questions are never appropriate at the interviewing stage, and they will be held against you in the evaluations. Moreover, in terms of informational value, these questions are worthless. Salary information for most firms is available online, and it may actually change before you start working.

Thanks to the popular legal blog Abovethelaw.com, there is such an abundance of salary and bonus information online that you would have to try hard not to find it. Furthermore, salary information may be available on the firm's Website or in the job description itself. Many firms mention that they pay "competitive salaries" or even list a possible salary range. Finally, most employers will state in their offer letters the salary they will pay you. If, after looking for a while, you still cannot find an answer, you may discuss compensation with your potential employer. However, only do so after you receive an offer. See Chapter 29 for further discussion of this topic.

"What is the quality of life here?"

This question is unoriginal and ambiguous and calls for a Pollyanna response about work-life balance. Even worse, it tells your interviewer you are not willing to work hard. We understand your predicament and your desire to get paid the highest market salary, do challenging, interesting work (none of that document review or due diligence stuff), and still be able to leave at 5 p.m. You must realize, however, that you will work hard no matter where you end up. BigLaw attorneys, small-firm attorneys, government lawyers, and even law clerks—the vast majority of them work hard. And those paid the highest salaries tend to work the most. It is therefore erroneous to assume that there is such a thing as a "lifestyle firm." Of course, all legal positions vary in the challenges you will face, the hours and number of weekends you must work, and the temperaments of your supervisors. But these things are often more a matter of luck than anything else, and you cannot scope out these facts merely by asking your interviewer about the quality of life at the firm.

> Our friends Albert and Jeff work at the same firm. Their offices are in the same building, and they do the same kind of work. Jeff gets to leave every day at 5:30 p.m. and does not work much on the weekends. Albert, however, never leaves before 8 p.m. and has to work almost every weekend. Thus, what is described as a "lifestyle firm" by Jeff is a "sweatshop" for Albert. The reason? Jeff got lucky and was paired up with two partners with small children who try not to work on the weekends. Meanwhile, Albert mostly works for an overachieving senior partner who believes weekends are like Santa (not real).

As discussed in Chapter 29, most lifestyle questions are appropriate at the post-offer stage, when you no longer risk losing an offer. If you are still tempted to ask these questions during an interview, ask carefully worded, focused questions designed to elicit helpful answers. What you do not want to do is ask questions that are too general or questions that clearly indicate you do not want to work hard. The former will call for an unhelpful "we are great" response; the latter may cost you an offer.

> Bruce, a partner at a medium-sized firm, complains that he is asked questions about lifestyle a little too often. If he could give the interviewees an honest response, here is what he would say: "Now let me get this straight: You have not done a day of legal work in your life, you are interviewing for a summer associate position in which you will be wined and dined and do virtually no work, and you actually want to know how little work you can get away with?"

There are several lifestyle questions you can ask without antagonizing your interviewer. For example, you can ask the junior attorneys if they are able to work from home on late nights and weekends. This question allows for two helpful answers: "Yes, I can work from home," or "Yes, but I hardly ever work nights and weekends." Of course, if it turns out that you must work at the office at all times, this will help dispel any notions you may have had about the quality of life at that firm. You can also ask whether the firm holds events or activities to facilitate attorney bonding, or whether your interviewer was able to take vacations last year. But, if you can help it, the best thing to do is to save the lifestyle questions for later.

Questions Containing Publicly Available Information

"How many lawyers does your firm have?" "How many lawyers in this office do IP?" "When did this office open?" "What practice areas is this office known for?" Here is what your interviewer is thinking when he or she hears these questions: "Are you kidding me? I have to waste .2 hours of my otherwise-billable time regurgitating publicly available information because you were either too lazy to Google it or cannot think of something better to ask? For that reason alone I don't want to hire you!" Most firms have Websites, which contain all kinds of useful information. There is also NALP, Vault.com, and other helpful resources that have answers to these questions. Use them first, and only ask your interviewer a question if the answer is not available anywhere else.

Additionally, remember to mention that you did all the groundwork before asking the question. This will convince your interviewer that you are serious about his or her firm and willing to invest time in research. Asking something such as, "I know that your firm's D.C. office has a large private equity group, but do they also do real estate work?" will ensure that you question will be received better than if you simply asked the interviewer to list all the practice groups in the D.C. office. Your mantra should be "research first, ask questions later."

Questions About Leave Policies

This goes hand-in-hand with the second question. Asking about whether you can take time off and still get paid before actually receiving an offer is just wrong. Resist this impulse entirely. These may be legitimate concerns for you, but at this point they are premature. You can always ask these questions once you receive an offer. For now, just assume that the firm's time-off policy is designed to make you feel guilty about leaving the office. Also assume that the firm's paid parental leave policy is in the neighborhood of 12 weeks. We cannot speak for all firms, but this is true for many of them. If your firm offers more than that, you will be pleasantly surprised later.

Questions About the Law

"So, what do you make of that Ninth Circuit ERISA decision?" or (worse yet) "Any thoughts about the legality of Israel's Separation Wall under international law?" Questions such as these tell your interviewer that either you are boring, you want to show off, or you do not really understand the legal issues involved.

Most lawyers do not casually talk about random legal issues in their spare time unless those issues directly pertain to their practice. Moreover, whatever you think you know about any given legal issue or controversy, a practicing attorney (especially one with experience in that field) will probably know much more, and your comments could easily betray your ignorance. You can also embarrass your interviewer if he or she has no idea what you are talking about. In short, these types of questions may turn out to have a much less impressive effect than you had hoped. Therefore, if you need to make conversation, rather than asking complex legal questions or attempting to show off your legal prowess, focus on something lighthearted and easy to discuss, such as hobbies, cooking, traveling, law school experience, and so on. If you claim to have a certain hobby, however, be prepared to show a genuine interest in that hobby.

> When Beverly's interviewer jokingly said he was looking for an associate who could bake, she informed him that, although she did not bake well, one of her passions was gourmet cooking. Intrigued, the interviewer asked follow-up questions. As it turned out, Beverly had exaggerated her cooking skills. When she was asked pointed questions, she revealed that her "passion" consisted of occasionally watching cooking shows and regularly dining at upscale restaurants. In other words, she herself did not do any gourmet cooking. Although she was otherwise a strong candidate, this seemingly innocent misrepresentation was enough to cost her an offer. Her interviewer was no longer confident that she had given him an accurate picture of her background.

Generic Gap-Filler Questions

When faced with an awkward silence during an interview, you may be tempted to keep the conversation going. Most interviewees resort to generic questions in order to fill the gaps—for example, "What are your hours like?" or "What kind of work do you do?" One candidate even asked why his interviewer decided to be a lawyer. Rather than fill awkward silences with random questions, you should have a list of good questions prepared in advance. Read Chapter 11 to help you come up with good questions for this occasion. If you must ask spontaneous questions, do your best to sound genuine. Better yet, instead of asking new questions, follow up on something the interviewer said earlier.

Of course, you should always try to save a few good questions for the end. But if you already asked well-thought-out questions during your interview, the interviewer is not going to hold it against you if you run out of questions. To improve your chances of an offer, simply say, "I have researched your firm very carefully and, even though I had several questions when I came in, you told me everything I wanted to know. Based on my research and your feedback, I am confident that this is a place where I want to work. Do you have any questions for me?" It often works like magic.

Questions About Firm Scandals

Questions about how a firm has dealt with racially offensive comments or insensitive employees may be legitimate. But, for your offer's sake, go easy with these types of questions. If you really must know an answer before deciding whether to join a firm, your law school career services may help by asking this question on behalf of the student body. Alternatively, if you are interviewing as a lateral attorney, try to find an insider within the firm who can give you straightforward answers without letting it affect your chances of an offer. The interview is not the right place to ask about firm scandals.

One year, a major international law firm experienced two cross-cultural scandals shortly before the interviewing season. First, one of its lawyers sent a firm-wide e-mail asking if anyone would like to adopt some puppies. A partner in that firm apparently replied (also in a firm-wide e-mail), "Please don't let these puppies go to a Chinese restaurant!" Next, when the firm's Hong Kong office closed down later that year, another attorney e-mailed everyone at the firm a music parody titled "So Solly" (to be sung to the tune of "Hello Dolly"). Rob had an interview with that firm. The interview was dry and boring, and Rob decided to spice things up. So, when the interviewer asked if Rob had any questions about the firm, guess what? Rob asked about the firm's lack of sensitivity toward Asians. The partner turned bright red and, clearly trying to contain his anger, replied that the firm was working on improving its image. Rob's phone was not ringing with a callback from this firm.

Also keep in mind that many firms have dirty laundry of some sort, and that the firm management and your interviewer cannot do much about those scandals. Do not automatically judge an entire firm based on rumors about one or more of its bad apples, and do not ask questions about scandals if you can help it.

Personal Questions

Although it may seem self-evident, we are including this advice because there are many job applicants who make the mistake of asking overly personal questions. Although it may be tempting to ask your interviewer personal questions, you should resist this temptation because you never know how your interviewer may react. Some interviewers are eager to talk about their children, their married lives, or their vacations. But others may be very offended if you try to solicit such information.

> A federal judge once rescinded an offer to her incoming law clerk because the clerk asked the judge if she was married. Never mind that the clerk asked this question a month before starting her clerkship, or that the question came up at an informal lunch with the judge. The judge was so taken aback by this question that she rescinded an offer on the spot.

There are a number of questions you should never ask your interviewers. These include questions about money, bonuses, parental leave, vacation policies, publicly available information, personal questions, and firm scandals. The wrong questions will tell the interviewer that you do not understand how the interviewing game works. Asking questions during an interview is one of many tests given to you by your potential employer, and you cannot flunk it. If something is really a concern, talk to your career counselors or your friends at the firm, or *maybe* ask the firm—but only after you get an offer.

QuickReview

✓ Your interviewers judge you by your questions, so choose them carefully.
✓ Prepare your questions in advance.
✓ Do not fill awkward silences with dull, unnecessary questions.
✓ Avoid questions about firm scandals, personal questions, and questions about the law.
✓ Do not ask about a firm's leave policy, compensation, or work-life balance until you receive an offer.
✓ Always try to put a positive spin on negative questions.
✓ Do not ask questions to which you should know the answers.

Chapter 10

LIMITED DISCLOSURE

Legal employers, especially firms, are reluctant to hire and train young lawyers who may subsequently leave them to pursue other opportunities. Therefore, they engage in careful screening in efforts to eliminate candidates who are flight risks. Although you may view certain topics as innocent conversation starters, interviewers may be using them to probe your true intentions. Accordingly, avoid discussing your plans for the future, volunteering personal information, or expressing an interest in such subjects as legal academia and public service.

Silence Is Golden

Although honesty is the best policy in most, if not all, spheres of everyday life, during legal interviews it can easily cost you an offer. If you can help it, do not disclose information that can be used against you to potential employers. Lying on a resume, concealing material information, making up fictitious ties to an area, or presenting someone else's writing sample as your own are wrong; but giving away information your interviewers can use to not hire you is not to your advantage, either.

When it comes to certain issues, the less you disclose, the better. For example, you do not want to disclose that you do not see yourself working at your target firm a few years down the road. Likewise, you do not want to reveal a lack of interest in the work the employer may ask you to do. Do not volunteer information about family issues, small children, or health problems. Say what the employer wants to hear while telling the truth, but without volunteering negative information.

> Chase applied for jobs in all major cities. Although he really wanted to practice in San Francisco, he did not get a single interview there. So he decided to work in New York

for a few years and try to relocate to San Francisco later. During his interviews with New York firms, he was asked repeatedly why he wanted to be in New York. If Chase had volunteered that he was using it as a stepping stone to get to California, he would have never gotten an offer. Instead, Chase replied that New York was a great city, and that he thought he would really enjoy living and working there. He told the truth without volunteering harmful information.

Location

It is easy to let your tongue slip and to reveal something you do not want an interviewer to know, such as your lack of interest in or ties to the area. This problem comes from being unprepared. When people are asked to discuss a subject that they are not ready or willing to discuss, they tend to panic. The result is that they reveal more than is necessary.

While interviewing for a summer associate position, Doug noted he wanted to end up at one of the large Southern cities. The interview took place in Jackson, Mississippi, and his interviewer could not help but wonder why Doug was looking at Jackson instead of cities such as New Orleans or Nashville. Doug's slipup made the interviewer realize that Doug did not have a genuine connection to or desire to work in Jackson. Instead, Doug simply thought he had a better shot at securing a summer position in a smaller town.

Demonstrating your ties to a location where you are looking for a job is extremely important. Lack of genuine ties to an area is the single most important reason why many employers reject qualified candidates. If you want to improve your chances, do not disclose anything that may indicate your lack of desire to stay in the area long-term.

Sasha revealed to the interviewer that she was a "small-town gal," but that she wanted to practice in New York for a few years to know what it feels like to be in a metropolitan area. The interviewer's impression was that Sasha was simply looking to get a few years of New York experience on her resume and then move back to her hometown. Sasha did not get an offer.

Summer Splits and Clerkships

Interviewers often trick job applicants into revealing their intentions by putting a positive spin on certain information. For example, they proudly tell the candidates that the firm encourages summer splits, gives associates unlimited credit for pro bono work, or allows them to move between offices. In addition to their marketing value, these statements help weed out those candidates who are too eager to take advantage of such opportunities. Summer splits and clerkships are some of the trickiest topics. Some firms strongly encourage them; others do not allow them at all. Unless you are certain that your firm would strongly encourage such an experience, do not discuss it during your interview.

Pro Bono Work

When it comes to discussing pro bono work, discuss it in moderation. Virtually all firms today do two things to make a difference: They go green, and they do pro bono. If you casually mention to the interviewer that you are interested in pro bono work, he or she will love you for it. The operative word here, however, is "casually." Although it is great to let the interviewer know that you are willing to do some pro bono work, it is never a good idea to portray your pro bono efforts as a mission. Partners are weary of associates who think they can work in a law firm, get paid an attorney's salary, and spend the vast majority of their time working for non-paying clients.

Just Don't Talk About It

Certain subjects should never be discussed during firm interviews. These subjects are parental leave and vacation, your desire to work in the public sector, and your interest in academia. Firms are reluctant to invest money in associates who may soon leave them. By disclosing even a remote interest in these opportunities, you are basically informing your interviewer that you are applying for a short-term job.

Post-Offer Discussions

Some of the topics in this chapter are fair game once you receive an offer. For example, you can ask about summer splits and clerkships, express an interest in working on pro bono cases, inquire about firm-sponsored opportunities to engage in public service, or ask about leave policies—but only *after* you get an offer. At this stage of the hiring process, the employer has invested sufficient resources and has come to like you. Accordingly, it may be more willing to accommodate your requests. Read Chapter 29 for tips on how to approach these discussions.

This chapter covers most of the major topics that should always be subject to limited disclosure. Of course, you may have additional concerns or issues not discussed here. The key to figuring out what not to discuss is to place yourself in the shoes of your interviewers. They want smart, hardworking people to devote all of their time and energy to working for them. Accordingly, avoid questions that signal that you would be less than 100 percent committed to this job. Tread lightly, and wait until the post-offer stage to discuss the issues that are important to you.

QuickReview

✓ Questions that signal that you are less than 100 percent committed to your future job may jeopardize your chances of getting an offer.

✓ If you indicate to your interviewer that your tenure may be short-lived, you are giving him or her a reason not to hire you.

✓ Although you should never lie in an interview, you do not necessarily have to disclose all your professional or personal hopes, dreams, and aspirations.

✓ Do your homework before discussing summer splits and clerkships, and always indicate your compatibility with a prospective employer's policies about these issues.

✓ Do not discuss public sector or academic aspirations at firm interviews.

✓ Ties to a geographic location are key for any job. Disclose your reasons for interviewing in a particular place, but do not volunteer information about your possible interest in other locations.

✓ Ask for information about parental leave, vacations, and other benefits only after receiving an offer.

Chapter 11

GAP-FILLERS FOR AWKWARD MOMENTS

Many candidates have experienced those awkward moments during job interviews when the conversation stops, and both the interviewer and the interviewee are desperately searching for a new topic. When this happens, you must re-engage the interviewer and take on the burden of carrying on the conversation. You can do this by following up on something the interviewer said earlier, by asking "gap-filler" questions, or by using other examples from this chapter. Most importantly, remember that good interviewees are also good listeners; if you listen to your interviewer carefully, you will have a number of follow-up questions at your disposal.

Focus on the Interviewer

Most lawyers are intelligent and accomplished, and they love to talk about themselves. So if you ask a flattering question about some aspect of their background, education, or experience, you will likely get a positive response. By focusing on your interviewers, you will help kill time, learn something about them, and make them feel good about themselves. The possibilities here are endless. If you did your homework, you should have no difficulty asking questions, such as, "So, I noticed that you are widely published in the area of antitrust law. How did you become interested in this area?" or "How did you decide to do pro bono work for the ACLU?"

Jessica found herself in an uncomfortable silence during her interview with a senior partner. She did not know much about him, but she recalled reading on his firm bio that he had argued and won numerous appeals before the Ninth Circuit. Because she did not remember details about the case, she asked a general gap-filler question: "So, what was it like to argue before the Ninth Circuit?" As it turned out, oral arguments were the highlight of this partner's legal career. Instantly melting, he told Jessica about his arguments and the fact that he won most of them. The interview took a pleasant turn, and Jessica no longer needed to resort to gap-fillers after asking this question.

Refrain From Humor

Your interviewer may crack a joke or two to lighten up the mood, and you had better laugh if you want an offer. But, as an interviewee, you should refrain from using humor during interviews.

Peter was in the middle of a very dry interview with Clarence Thomas's former clerk. Trying to impress the interviewer with his great sense of humor, Peter said, "You know, I met Justice Thomas once at a law school event. Unfortunately, I really didn't talk to him much, as he was mostly interested in talking to the ladies there." The interviewer got up, silently walked to the door, and said to Peter, "Let me take you to your next interview. I have no more questions."

By cracking jokes in such a formal setting, you risk antagonizing the person who has the power to give you a job. Remember that even if your friends find you exceptionally witty, your interviewers may find your jokes boring or, worse, offensive.

Terry, a UNC Law grad, made a futile attempt at humor during his callback interview. While discussing UNC basketball with a female partner, Terry told her a story about a UNC vs. Maryland game he recently attended. Being a loyal UNC fan, Terry apparently had held up a "Maryland has crabs" sign during the game. "Oh, I love crabs," exclaimed the interviewer. She paused for a second—and then gave Terry a horrid look. To say the interview was mildly uncomfortable from that point on would be an understatement.

This is a risk you do not want to take during your job search. So the rule of thumb here is do not try to make them laugh, and laugh with them but never at them. Now, if the interviewer asks you a humorous gap-filler question, then you can score points by giving a witty answer.

When Gary's interviewer ran out of topics of conversation, he asked Gary what he would do if he woke up one day to find 50 million dollars in his bank account. "I would ask where the other 50 million went!" replied Gary. Gary's witty reply was a good icebreaker and showed that he would be a fun person to work with.

Examples of Gap-Fillers

"But what do I ask about? This guy is pretty boring," you may say. Not to worry. Here is a sample list of tried and proven gap-fillers:

Example 1: "You appear to have developed a niche in securities law, which does not seem to be an area someone just falls into. What drew you to this practice?" This question is safe for firm interviews because most senior lawyers at firms have narrow specialization; because they are proud of the fact that they are experts in a specific area; and because law firms often encourage young associates to develop a specialty, because it is very lucrative for law firms and valuable to their clients. Therefore, unless your interviewer does general litigation or a broad variety of corporate work (which is becoming rare, especially at large firms), this is a good question. It is also one that your interviewer will enjoy answering.

Example 2: "What kind of work do you expect an associate in your group to perform in the first two years of practicing at the firm, and what type of skills would you like to see him or her develop?" This is a good question because it is useful for you to know what would be expected of you, and it shows your interviewer that you mean business and are serious in trying to prepare for this job and your career.

Example 3: "Is that your son playing soccer in the photo? I love soccer. I was on a team myself when I was in college. How long has he been playing?" You should scan your interviewer's office for sports memorabilia, awards of any kind, or any other hints of a personality. Then feel free to ask a question similar to this one. Anything an attorney hangs in his or her office is something he or she is proud of. And do not worry that you are moving away from a discussion of law- or firm-related issues. Sometimes, talking about something other than the law is a welcome break. But, of course, avoid questions that are too personal.

Example 4: "I noticed from your profile that you volunteer for Habitat for Humanity. How did you get involved?" If you have time to review the interviewer's bio, you can earn major points by asking him or her about major achievements, key clients, community involvement, or pro bono work.

Example 5: "I want to work at a firm that allows its associates to perform some pro bono work. What type of pro bono work has your office been involved with?" Many firms devote significant resources to pro bono work and are not shy about using this

fact in their recruiting materials. Most interviewers, therefore, will eagerly talk about the firm's pro bono efforts. Just
be sure to read Chapter 10 to ensure you phrase your question correctly.

Whatever you choose as your gap-filler, try to direct the conversation
toward a topic in which you are genuinely interested. Good gap-filler questions will not only help you kill time, but they will help you learn something interesting and useful about your potential employer. Do your
homework, listen carefully to what your interviewer and his or her bio
have to say, and you will be armed with plenty of gap-filler questions for
your interview.

QuickReview

✓   The need for gap-fillers may arise because the interviewer is tired,
    is a poor communicator, or is unprepared, or simply because you
    have nothing in common.
✓   Think of gaps in an interview as an opportunity to learn some-
    thing interesting or to flatter the interviewer.
✓   You can either come up with new questions or follow up on some-
    thing the interviewer had said previously.
✓   Do your homework so that you have enough information at your
    disposal to ask good gap-filler questions.
✓   Scan the interviewer's office and ask about something that illus-
    trates his or her personality.
✓   If you have nothing else to ask, ask traditional gap-filler ques-
    tions about the interviewer's specialty, your future job responsi-
    bilities, or the firm's pro bono work.
✓   Remember, this is your opportunity to distinguish yourself by
    being an engaging conversationalist. So think of some good gap-
    fillers in advance.

Chapter 12

Answering Inappropriate or Illegal Questions

Illegal or inappropriate questions and remarks are surprisingly common during legal interviews, considering that such interviews are conducted by lawyers. It appears that no amount of sensitivity training can do away with them completely. Although it is impossible (and unnecessary) to list all different examples of illegal or inappropriate questions, there are two basic types: First, there are the blatantly illegal and discriminatory questions and remarks (intentional or not); second, there are questions that are obviously inappropriate or offensive, but not necessarily illegal. Your job as the interviewee is to recognize these questions for what they are and decide on your feet how to deal with them—hopefully to your advantage.

Illegal and Discriminatory Questions

On the one end of the spectrum, some interviewers may ask questions that are illegal. These have to do with how you have benefited from affirmative action, your plans to have children, or your reasons for belonging to a minority organization. When it comes to such illegal questions and remarks, we have seen it all. There was the infamous comment to a student of a Lebanese origin about "those Ay-rabs," and a lengthy diatribe about the sinfulness of gay marriage to a student who had clearly noted on his resume that he belonged to an LGBT association. Or what about the interviewer who asked an Albanian student whether she could do something to get rid of her "distracting" accent, or the interviewer who actually asked an African-American candidate whether she was "really a minority" because of the light color of her skin. And then there was a student who had her offer withdrawn after she told the firm she was pregnant. ("We hired you for a summer associate position, and because you are due in the middle of the summer, there was never a meeting of the minds.")

Of course, whether a given question is illegal or not may depend on the context in which it is asked. If a hiring partner jokingly asks a very tall Caucasian male candidate whether he went to his Big 10 school on a basketball scholarship, such a question may well be innocuous. On the other hand, if a similar question is asked of an African-American applicant of any height, it would be borderline illegal at best.

Most law firms that regularly recruit new attorneys have annual "refreshers" at the beginning of their recruiting season, in which either a human resources manager or an employment lawyer reminds the interviewers about their guidelines for asking questions. In general, questions that should not be asked under any circumstances include those pertaining to a candidate's race, religion, nationality, age, gender, sexual orientation, and family status, as well as any other characteristics that have no relation to any bona fide job qualification. No matter how diligent their efforts, however, there are always a few bad apples who just do not learn.

> During an interview with a "family-oriented" firm, the hiring partner asked Ursula about her American-sounding last name (Ursula had an obvious German accent). Unprepared for this question, Ursula admitted that this was her married name. Seeing this as an invitation to pry, the partner proceeded to ask about her husband, whether they had children, and whether her parental responsibilities would allow her to join a busy law practice. Ursula explained that she was once married but was now divorced, and a single mother to a small child. A week later she received a rejection from the firm. The letter came as a shock to her and everyone else—Ursula was bright, personable, and at the top of her class at a good law school. In fact, every other employer she interviewed with had made her an offer. Ursula got suspicious and did some digging. Through a contact at the firm, she found out that the firm did not hire her because of her "family issues." Of course, it was improper for the partner to ask about her family, even though technically she "volunteered" she had one. But it was her honest answer that cost her an offer.

Inappropriate Questions

On the other end of the spectrum are questions that are inappropriate or just plain awkward. Perhaps the interviewer is dying to ask a question he or she understands may be illegal, but asks it anyway in a more oblique fashion. One African-American applicant interviewed with a partner who "casually" asked her about her dress style. The interviewee got suspicious and asked the partner to elaborate. As it turned out, the firm had previously hired a female African-American associate whose dress style, they felt, was "inappropriate." The interviewer awkwardly explained that the firm wanted to avoid this "problem" with future African-American job applicants.

Most questions fall into the gray area between illegality and inappropriateness. For example, during an interview at a well-known D.C. firm, an older, seasoned partner asked a female candidate whether she planned to have a family in the near future. He explained that it was a major financial burden for the firm to have to retain women attorneys who later got married, had babies, and quit their jobs. The partner appeared genuinely disheartened that a particular female associate he had taken under his wing, and who had stellar partnership prospects, had left the firm to raise her young children. He went on and on about all the money, time, and resources spent on training this young associate. The candidate, it turned out, was gay. She assured the partner she was gay and had no imminent plans to marry or have children. After an awkward silence, the partner told her that she "might consider" another prominent firm, which, he said, was known for hiring gay attorneys.

So how do you deal with these very awkward and potentially difficult situations? "To hell with you and your racist, sexist, bigoted firm," you may (justifiably) want to say in response to any of the previous examples. As an educated person expecting civility and fairness from your future employer and colleagues, you may well be entitled to such righteous indignation. But as a lawyer interviewing for a job in a competitive market, you don't always have this luxury. You must first think of the consequences of your reaction and consider your options. Regardless of whether a question is illegal or just inappropriate, you generally have the following options to choose from.

Option 1: Ask the interviewer to elaborate

It is possible that your interviewer has a legitimate reason to ask a seemingly inappropriate question. Perhaps he or she asked you about your age because he or she realized that you share a hometown and wants to find out if you went to the same high school. Asked in these circumstances, a question about your age does not justify overreacting and jeopardizing your chances. If you are unsure about a question, you can ask the interviewer to elaborate, which will give him or her a chance to explain or retract the question, and shift the interview to a more positive mood. Just do this in a neutral, nonthreatening tone.

Option 2: Say nothing and take one on the chin

As much as it pains us to say this, the safest option in terms of optimizing your chances for an offer is to allow the question. This is especially true if you really need the job and want to maximize your chances of getting it. If you can satisfy the interviewer's sick curiosity and tell him or her what he or she wants to hear, your chances of an offer will significantly improve. If you think an honest answer will help you, go ahead and volunteer the information. Otherwise, a rebuttal, a joke, or some other form of diversion is best. Try to anticipate the insensitive questions your background could inspire. When you get an offer, of course, you can judge for yourself whether you actually want to work there.

> During her on-campus interview, Kayla met with a senior partner and an associate from a prominent firm. Both men were alums from Kayla's law school, and the conversation touched upon such topics as favorite classes and professors. Kayla, who was applying to the firm's bankruptcy department, asked them if they knew Professor Cox, who had been teaching bankruptcy at this school for the last 20 years. The partner then asked Kayla why she was interested in practicing bankruptcy law. She gave a thoughtful and detailed answer, and concluded by saying, "I just really like bankruptcy law." "So, what you are saying is that you really like Cox," stated the partner, winking at his colleague. Both men laughed hysterically. Although Kayla could have walked out, she chose to resort to humor instead. "Of course," she enthusiastically replied, as if oblivious to the inappropriate implication, "doesn't everyone?"

How you react to inappropriate questions is not just important for the sake of getting an offer; your reaction can also have a lasting effect on your legal career. As a lawyer, your reputation is your most precious asset. Never jeopardize it by giving a hasty response to a bad question.

Option 3: Answer the question and go on the offensive

This is a somewhat risky option. But it may work for those who want to acknowledge the elephant in the room and still to have a shot at getting an offer. When asked if being a foreigner means you have poor writing skills, consider answering, "I am confident that I will be a highly effective writer, as indicated by my top grade in legal writing class, my membership on the law review, and my high class ranking. In addition, I do not think my national origin or ethnic background should preclude me from working as a lawyer." When asked if being a single mother will interfere with your work, consider the following response: "As a single mother, I always make my employer's needs a priority, because my employer allows me to support my child and pay for her private school, which is important for her future. It's always been that way, and she understands it."

Answers such as these do two things: First, they help you put your best foot forward in terms of your qualifications. Second, terms such as "single mother," "national origin," "ethnic background," and "preclude" will hopefully set off an alarm in your interviewer's head and remind him or her to be politically correct. This is one way to answer an improper question and put pressure on your interviewer to give you an offer.

Option 4: Refuse to answer

Of course, you can simply state, "I will not answer that question," or "I believe this question is inappropriate [or illegal]." This is an easy way out of a difficult situation, but it is hardly a practical one. Such a reaction will likely ruin any chances you had with this employer, especially if you misunderstood the question.

Option 5: Report the conduct

Resorting to this option will likely mean losing any chance you had of getting an offer. Unfortunately, this is the sad reality of the legal market. Once you tell your career services, they may feel obligated to confront the employer. Firm management will then contact the interviewer, who will, without a doubt, recall your specific interview. They will then find a way not to hire you. A rebuke by a law school administration can have a powerful impact on a firm's future interviewing and hiring practices, but you will not enjoy the benefits of this reform because you will likely never have a future at that firm. There is a slim chance that they will still give you an offer, but it is unlikely. The damage to their reputation will have already been done by your reporting, and they will have little to gain from hiring you.

If you decide to contact the media, insist on anonymity. In the past few years, law blogs and mainstream media have featured numerous stories about law students who complained to career services, wrote letters to newspapers, sent school-wide notices, or e-mailed the firm's management about what they felt was inappropriate behavior during interviews. But even when a firm took proactive steps and apologized for the incident, the student in question received plenty of bad publicity, as well. In many cases, the student's name was circulated on the Web, searchable and identifiable by all potential employers.

> A Dallas partner had the misfortune of making a racial comment during his on-campus interview with an African-American student. Specifically, while reciting verbatim testimony from a civil rights case he worked on, the partner dropped the N-word. It did not matter that the partner himself was an African-American, or that the comment was not meant as derogatory. Deeply offended, the student reported the incident to

career services. The partner received a slap on the wrist from the firm's management. The firm publicly apologized for the incident. The law school barred the firm from interviewing on campus the next year. The story made national news. Luckily, the student was smart enough to speak out anonymously, which shielded his identity from the mainstream media.

Option 6: File a lawsuit

Filing a lawsuit may also be an option. Consult a lawyer if you feel the situation warrants this, but be very careful: Employers are reluctant to hire lawyers with a litigious history. Remember the widely publicized employment discrimination lawsuits filed by lawyers? Where are these lawyers now? We do not know, either. So think twice before resorting to litigation.

Our Advice

If you end up in hot water with your interviewer, we urge you to cool off before taking action. Make sure that your response is dispassionate and carefully worded. Before reporting the conduct—and risking losing an offer—consider whether the incident is worth it. If you feel a reaction is necessary, consult someone first. If you do decide to go public, do so anonymously. Although the interviewer will know who leaked the information, it may not go any further than that. Meanwhile, hopefully you will make enough noise to get the issue addressed.

Although most employers educate their interviewers about illegal or inappropriate interviewing behavior, you are still likely to encounter it. No one should ever have to anticipate such questions, but if you want to maximize your career opportunities, it is to your benefit to have a game plan. Consider the options presented in this chapter, anticipate discriminatory or inappropriate questions in light of your particular background, and always stay calm. Your goal is to have a maximum number of offers to choose from, rather than to simply put your interviewer in his or her place. You can always turn down an offer from an interviewer who was acting inappropriately, but it is good to have options first.

QuickReview

✓   Prior to the interview, consider what in your background could prompt illegal or inappropriate questions, and decide ahead of time how you will react.

✓   Make sure your reaction is the product of calm, rational thinking about your career goals and the ramifications of your response.
✓   Consider the options discussed in this chapter and determine what option is best for your particular situation.

Part III

❦

Interviewing Etiquette Do's and Don'ts

Chapter 13

BOLD MOVES

By the time you are interviewing, you cannot change much about your resume. Your grades are what they are, as are your extracurricular activities, journal membership, law school, and employment history. But what you do have control over is you. As you prepare for your interviews, you may find it helpful to evaluate your candidacy from the employer's perspective. Put yourself in your interviewer's shoes. During on-campus interviews, for example, interviewers meet 12 to 20 candidates a day, with only a few short breaks in between. As you can imagine, by the end of the day, the interviewers are exhausted. It is not surprising then that to the interviewers, most of the students blend into one faceless candidate with rather unremarkable credentials. What this means is that only those candidates who can distinguish themselves are able to move on to the next level. Therefore, you must do your best not to blend in with the reject crowd.

Make a Lasting Impression

Say you walk into an interview room late in the afternoon. Of course, if you have already read Chapter 2, you will know that this is not the best time to schedule an interview; you will leave a more lasting impression if you interview early in the morning when the interviewer's memory is still fresh. But sometimes you have no choice.

As you are walking in, you immediately notice that your interviewer is already crashing from his or her morning caffeine high and is barely paying any attention to you or the surroundings. Without looking up from his BlackBerry, he nods with complete disinterest as you introduce yourself. He then asks you a generic and hopelessly uninspiring question such as, "So, what can I tell you about my firm?" In this all-too-common scenario, you have only two options. One option is to play it safe, make the best of a dry interview, try to look excited as you exchange meaningless questions and answers, and hope for the best. Another option is to try something different that will leave a memorable impression.

Transform a dry interview into an engaging one

Here are a few examples of how actual interviewees managed to transform a dry and boring interview into an engaging conversation and a post-interview callback.

> Jeremy was a typical law student going through his interviews without much luck. He attended a second-tier school, was not on a journal, and had average grades. Potential employers were less than enthusiastic about his candidacy. Only two firms invited him to interview. To make matters worse, his interview with one of these firms was scheduled for 5 p.m., the last interview that day. But Jeremy decided to give it his best shot. So he showed up to the interview with two cans of beer in hand. After the tired-looking interviewer greeted him, Jeremy said, "I know you've had long a day, so I thought you could use a cold one." The interviewer laughed, and they had a relaxing and enjoyable conversation over a beer. When the interviewer recommended this candidate for a callback, the hiring partner was puzzled by his choice, as Jeremy clearly did not meet the firm's GPA criteria. Without going into too much detail (for obvious reasons), the interviewer explained that Jeremy simply had "a winning personality."

Naturally, offering an interviewer a beer is a risky proposition, and we are not endorsing it. But it worked for Jeremy, who had nothing to lose to begin with, and who was rewarded for his daring attitude and entrepreneurial spirit with a callback.

> Anna had a more conservative approach. Her interview was scheduled for early in the morning. When she showed up for her interview, she noted that the interviewer was barely awake and still battling jetlag. So she offered to take him to the cafeteria for coffee. This gesture was very much appreciated by her interviewer. More importantly, it made the interview more casual and enjoyable for both of them. Anna also received a callback, even though her grades were slightly below the firm's cut-off point.

We have recommended this approach to many candidates, and, in every instance, the interviewers loved their morning coffee and thanked the candidates profusely.

> Alex used a similar technique. But instead of taking his interviewers to the cafeteria, he brought hot coffee to his morning interviews. His bold move was a big hit, as interviewers generally do not have time for a break or a refill, and the coffee was a real mood cure during the long interviewing process. Alex received several callbacks and eventually received an offer from a great firm.

If you decide to follow Alex's lead, make sure to also bring a few packs of sugar and cream. Some interviewers may get grumpy if they do not get their coffee sweet and light!

Another way to stand out is by being genuine. For example, when asked why you decided to go to law school, instead of offering some sob story about how you wanted to fight injustice, you can honestly say that you wanted a lucrative, stable profession. You may find that the attorneys you meet will relate better to an honest answer to this type of question.

> For Mario, being genuine was the key with an interviewer who looked very sleep deprived and disinterested. During an especially boring part of the interview, Mario asked, "Do you really enjoy what you do? Honestly?" His demeanor must have seemed genuine and his question sincere because the interviewer, after pondering this for a bit, said, "Honestly, there was a time when I did. I don't anymore." She then offered her candid impression of the legal profession and its woes. The genuineness of that conversation made the interview a positive experience for both of them.

Mario's move set him apart and helped him get a callback from this interviewer, but a question soliciting a more positive response would have been even better. You should always try to keep the conversation during interviews as positive as possible. Human psychology works in mysterious ways. Interviewers are less likely to react positively to interviewees who bring up a negative topic. Consequently, even the most engaging conversation will hurt your chances of an offer if it leaves your interviewer with a negative feeling.

> This advice worked well for Erin, a Tulane Law grad interviewing for a clerkship shortly after Hurricane Katrina. When the judge asked her how the hurricane affected her life, she placed a positive spin on her story. She acknowledged that it was a difficult time for everyone, but noted that she was able to reconnect with several members of her family shortly

> after the hurricane and felt lucky because they were safe. Erin then quickly shifted the conversation to another subject. The judge later told her he was impressed with her ability to respond in such a positive manner to such an emotionally charged question.

Finally, the most positive thing you can do is tell your interviewer that you have thoroughly researched the firm, that the firm is absolutely your first choice, and that you will accept on the spot if you receive an offer. Interviewers who routinely meet candidates who are uncertain about what they want to do and where they want to work will appreciate this kind of enthusiasm and commitment.

Weighing your options

Candidates who are different, genuine, entertaining, or just plain bold often make the most lasting impression on their interviewers. But it is also important not to be outrageous or obnoxious, and to apply a basic cost-benefit analysis to each of your interviews. If your chances of having a good interview and getting a callback or an offer appear good (based on your grades and judging by how your interview began), perhaps you should not try anything risky. If, on the other hand, your interview is going poorly, the interviewer seems to be going through the motions, or you have little to lose, then by all means be bold.

Do not be afraid to be bold. When you are lost in the interviewing crowd, the things that make you stand out could be the things that get the employer to notice you and give you a chance. Because lawyers (and, hence, law students) have a reputation of being risk averse, it may pay to break this stereotype and take some risk by trying something different during your interviews. Nevertheless, be careful when applying this advice beyond on-campus interviews. During callbacks, government, clerkship, and lateral interviews, your approach to interviewing must be much more subtle and conservative.

QuickReview

✓ Your goal during interviews is to stand out from the crowd.

✓ If your interview starts out as dry and boring, seek to transform it.

✓ Consider asking unusual questions, giving honest answers, and discussing non-legal issues.

✓ Do a cost-benefit analysis to help you decide whether to try a bold move at an interview.

✓ Generally, bold moves are good if you have nothing to lose, or if the interview is so boring that it is unlikely you will receive a callback or an offer otherwise.

✓ If the interview is engaging and is going well, or if you are a strong candidate, consider forgoing bold moves.

✓ Whatever you do, do not overdo it, and do not be arrogant.

Chapter 14

RUDE BEHAVIOR

Lawyers are prone to rude behavior, so you are bound to encounter it at least once during your interviews. If you feel that a question or remark is inappropriate, remember to respond in a calm manner. Read Chapter 12 to help you plan your reaction to rude behavior. At the same time, learn to distinguish between rudeness and legitimate work-related situations. For example, always be accepting of an interviewer's need to answer the phone or talk briefly with his or her colleague. You will gain a great deal from the interview by being respectful and understanding.

Interviewers Behaving Badly

Rude behavior during an interview is rather common. Sometimes it consists simply of the interviewer interrupting the candidate, talking too much about him- or herself, and/or not giving the interviewee an opportunity to discuss his or her skills. Sometimes it involves asking inappropriate questions, making rude comments, or engaging in discriminatory behavior. Interviewers are also known to interrupt interviews to take a phone call, check their BlackBerries, and even respond to e-mails. Although junior interviewers are generally more polite (and also less likely to receive important calls), sometimes they can be just as rude as their senior colleagues.

> Cindy once had a callback interview with a mid-level associate who told her he did not understand how Cindy got a callback. He proceeded to criticize her resume and disparage her law school grades. When his phone rang, he told Cindy he had to take it and proceeded to talk about random personal matters while she was still in the interviewing room. In short, he did not bother to make an impression because he had decided Cindy would never get an offer from the firm.

How to react to rude behavior

Your reaction to your interviewer's rude behavior is very important. Lawyers must learn to grow a thick skin, and some employers purposefully engage in rude behavior during interviews in an effort to weed out sensitive candidates. Sometimes the worst thing you can do is complain. Before acting upset, better be sure you are ready to give up an offer from this employer. Calling out the interviewer on his or her rude behavior may feel good, but it will not further your candidacy.

> Shortly before Glen's on-campus interview was scheduled to start, an interviewer emerged to inform him that it would be starting late because he was on the phone with an important client. When he finally ended his phone conversation, there were only five minutes remaining before the next interview was supposed to start. The interviewer thus decided to cut Glen's interview short in order to stay on schedule. Despite only having five minutes of one-on-one time with his interviewer, Glen was enthusiastic about the job. He quickly proceeded to list the key reasons why he deserved a callback. Impressed by Glen's behavior (and likely feeling guilty for cutting the interview short), the interviewer gave him a callback on the spot.

No matter how badly an interview is going, try to approach it with an open mind. Many things may change between the time you encounter rude behavior and receive an offer. You may reevaluate your priorities, discover you overreacted, or decide it was not a big deal after all. Moreover, you may be pleasantly surprised by the firm's friendly culture during the second round of interviews. It is always good to give your interviewer and his or her employer a second chance.

If the interviewer's phone rings, acknowledge this by asking politely if he or she needs to take it and by indicating you do not mind waiting. Understand that the pressure of billable hours and increasingly demanding clients often means that attorneys do not have the luxury of ignoring phone calls or not responding to e-mails right away. Instead of getting offended, make the best of the time you have. Finally, keep in mind that lawyers sometimes get so preoccupied with their work that they unintentionally ignore an interviewee. If this happens, it is fine to ask if the interviewer would prefer to reschedule. Just do not overreact and ruin your chances simply because you think someone may be acting rudely.

> Fred was excited about his lateral interview with a named firm partner. But when he arrived to the interview, he was forced to wait. The interviewer acknowledged Fred

when he was escorted into his office but continued to talk on the phone. After 15 minutes went by, Fred grew impatient. When the partner finally hung up the phone and turned to his e-mail, Fred lost it. As he stormed out of the interviewer's office, the recruiting coordinator ran up to him to ask why he was rushing out. "I have seen everything I need to see to know—I don't want to work here," he replied. The named partner, who was completely immersed in an urgent issue he was trying to resolve, was clueless about what had just happened.

Things not to do

As an interviewee, you must also be careful not to exhibit rude behavior yourself. Do not talk too much about things that preoccupy you but bore your interviewer. Do not be late, and do not appear distracted. And it should go without saying that you should keep your cell phone and BlackBerry turned off at all times. Because vibrating cell phones can be just as distracting as those that ring, do not use the vibrating function either. And, of course, if your cell rings during an interview because you forgot to turn it off, apologize and turn it off immediately.

Cory had an interview with a partner and an associate. The interview was going well, and the offer was forthcoming—until the phone rang. It was Cory's cell phone. This alone would be enough to not receive an offer at some conservative firms. But the story did not end there. Cory got up, informed the interviewers he had to take it, and walked out, leaving them utterly speechless. He returned a few minutes later, and, although he apologized, he never offered any explanation for his behavior. One of the interviewers later remarked, "Let's hope that phone call was informing him of an offer, because we are certainly not giving him one."

If for some compelling reason you must answer a call during an interview (and we cannot think of a good reason short of news of the birth of your child), keep it brief and apologize profusely. After taking the call, you had better have a good explanation for your behavior ("It's a boy!").

If you go through several rounds of interviews, at least one of them is likely to be interrupted with phone calls, e-mails, or other urgent communications directed at your interviewer. It is a fact of life because lawyers are very busy people. Expect it, and when it happens, graciously pause and ask the interviewer if he or she needs to take the call. Realize that interruptions are not personal affronts—they just happen. However, as an interviewee, never let your cell phone, BlackBerry, or any other gadget interrupt the interview.

QuickReview

✓ The legal profession is demanding, and interruptions are bound to happen during interviews.

✓ Be gracious and politely ask your interviewers whether they need to take the call.

✓ Likewise, if someone walks into the room during the interview, let the interviewer know you do not mind waiting or taking a break.

✓ Try not to judge the firm or the interviewer based on your brief interaction with them.

✓ Remember to turn off your cell phone, BlackBerry, and any other electronic gadgets during an interview.

✓ If your gadget rings, beeps, or vibrates, remember to apologize.

Chapter 15

Discussing Law, Politics, and Religion

Confirmation hearings are the rare occasions when you get your money's worth for that C-SPAN subscription; they make for good entertainment. As you are watching the nominees attempt to dodge questions about abortion, prayer in schools, and torture, remember that they must answer these questions due to the nature of their future positions. You, however, are not preparing for a confirmation hearing, just a job interview. Having certain political or religious views is not a part of your future job description, so it is best to avoid controversial subjects. Even if you have absolutely nothing else to talk about with your interviewer, pick another topic. Talk about the weather, hobbies, or gourmet cooking, if you wish, but stay away from highly charged, controversial issues.

Dodge the Interviewer's Questions

What do you do if the interviewer asks you about your views on these subjects? Because most legal employers remind their interviewers to stay away from controversial interview questions, your chances of encountering them are slim. Nevertheless, these questions still come up. Usually, they are not a test of your ability to be a lawyer; rather, they sometimes arise when the interviewer runs out of questions, or when he or she is curious about your background.

Even seemingly innocent questions or comments about controversial issues present an unparalleled opportunity for you to mess up. So, unless the interviewer asks you directly to share your views, avoid making opinionated comments or taking a position. Do not accept the interviewer's statements as an invitation to share your own views! If, for example, your interviewer held a political post or argued a religious freedom case in the past, do not feel compelled to respond in any way other than demonstrating admiration for his or her success.

> Ben was asked about religion because he listed on his resume his affiliations with Jewish organizations and the fact that he is fluent in Hebrew. Instead of simply acknowledging that he was of a Jewish heritage, Ben tried to diffuse the situation by a humorous comment. "Well, I am pretty Jewish," Ben said. "But then, I just had a double bacon cheeseburger before the interview, so I guess that makes me less kosher." Little did Ben know that his interviewer was Jewish himself. By making this unsolicited comment, Ben took a risk of antagonizing an interviewer who could otherwise have been his biggest ally.

In the unlikely event your interviewer asks point blank about your thoughts on abortion or elections, then you are obviously expected to answer. In this scenario, your interviewer expects you to take a position and to give a persuasive answer. Remember, however, that this is not an invitation for passionate advocacy. Give an answer that does not attempt to evade the question, but indicates respect for opposite views.

If you are unsure about the question or want to buy yourself some time, ask the interviewer to clarify the question. If you want to lighten up the mood, smile and ask, "Is this a test?" and proceed to give your answer. When giving an answer, instead of being cynical, critical, or one-sided, present both sides of the arguments fairly. ("Well, on the one hand, there is a moral obligation to protect the rights of the unborn child. On the other hand, a woman's privacy is a fundamental right.") Then take a position, saying something to the effect of, "Personally, I believe in X." An answer like this demonstrates an understanding of the subject, your ability to weigh both sides of an argument, and good lawyering skills. If you have not learned to do this in law school, promptly ask your school for a refund.

Do Not Volunteer Information

One of the most common requests during interviews is "Tell me about yourself." This request is an invitation to discuss your qualifications, background, and personality traits in two to three sentences. It is *not* an invitation to discuss your entire bio, affiliations, or views on controversial subjects. Likewise, if the interviewer shares his or her views or beliefs with you, do not treat this as an invitation to discuss your own views on the same subject.

> While discussing her leadership skills during an interview, Kellie said that she aspired to follow Obama's leadership style because she believed Obama was "good at delegating." She remarked that Hillary Clinton's "micromanaging" style did not appeal to her at all. Guess where her interviewer stood on politics? He was a strong Hillary supporter, which made the rest of the interview very uncomfortable.

You may belong to the ACLU, volunteer at a local church, or be a political activist on the side, but during your interview, these activities are virtually irrelevant, as they have no bearing on your ability to be a good lawyer. In some cases, they may be a distraction to the interviewer. Therefore, resist the urge to divulge information about your club memberships, your bumper stickers, or how you voted in the recent elections.

Never Take an Extreme Position

Whatever position you take on a given issue, no matter how sensitive or controversial it is, is fine. Chances are, at least some people share it. However, your view and explanation of your position must be reasonable and dispassionate. It is perfectly fine to say you are pro-life if asked; calling doctors who perform abortions "baby killers," however, is not. Lawyers, especially good ones, like to think that they understand and respect both sides of an argument. Show them that you can do the same.

Do Not Judge a Book by Its Cover

When you research your interviewer's bio, do not assume that because he or she went to a certain school or has a certain political affiliation, you know what his or her political leanings really are.

> During her clerkship interview with a George W. Bush appointee, Carol made it a point to share her strong conservative views with the judge. As it turned out, however, the judge was a very liberal judicial activist. Although he enjoyed hiring clerks with diverse political opinions, he did not hire Carol because he felt her views were too extreme.

Additionally, just because you know about your interviewer's views, do not assume he or she wants yours to be the same. Some judges, for example, intentionally hire clerks who have the opposite political beliefs of their own because they want to be able to gauge different views on key issues. So during clerkship interviews, it is fine to respectfully disagree with your interviewers, provided you do not take extreme positions. Likewise, interviewers with strong religious beliefs do not necessarily want to hire only those candidates who share their beliefs. So be respectful of others' choices, but be who you are.

Steer clear from discussing religion, politics, law, or other controversial issues during interviews. Because you never know in advance what kind of answer your interviewer expects, the safest option is to talk about innocuous topics such as weather, travel, work, or hobbies. Furthermore, do not assume that your interviewer wants you to express a certain view or to agree with his or her stand on the issue. Sometimes, an interviewer may be looking for someone who can give a genuine answer or even challenge his or her position. If you are asked to share your views, answer the question, but make sure your answer is balanced and dispassionate. Demonstrate your ability to appreciate both sides of an argument.

QuickReview

✓   Never bring up controversial issues during an interview.
✓   If the interviewer volunteers information about his or her views or beliefs, do not take this as an invitation to discuss your own.
✓   If the interviewer asks you directly about your stand on a certain issue, give a clear answer, but keep it brief and well-reasoned.
✓   Try to address both sides of an argument, and never take an extreme position.
✓   Do not make any assumptions about the interviewer's views.
✓   Sometimes an interviewer actually wants to hear the other side of the story, so it is okay to respectfully disagree with him or her.

Chapter 16

DEALING WITH ARROGANT INTERVIEWERS

"Why aren't your grades better?" "Is this the best law school you could get into?" "What makes you think you can be a lawyer?" Such interview questions are not uncommon. Successful attorneys are extremely smart and accomplished, and many are not shy about showing it. However, their success depends on junior associates who do all the grunt work and bill the hours. Some seasoned attorneys resent this dependency, especially in light of constantly rising associate salaries and cushy parental leave policies. Psychoanalysis aside, however, it does not really matter why your interviewer is rude or obnoxious. What matters is your reaction to this behavior, which will determine whether or not you will get the offer.

What Rudeness Looks Like

Interviewers can sometimes be rude to candidates. Here are a just few examples of the horror stories shared by the readers of the popular law blog AbovetheLaw.com:

Once, when I was interviewing on-campus back in law school, the partner assigned to interview me was on the phone when our interview was about to start. I knocked on the door, and he asked me to wait outside. *Not a problem*, I thought. *Perhaps it is a client emergency.* But as I stood outside, I could not help but overhear (this guy was loud) that the conversation was a casual discussion of a basketball game from the night before. *Perhaps he is discussing basketball with a client*, I thought, searching for an appropriate explanation. After the conversation was over, and the partner finally asked me to come inside, it was already 15 minutes into our 20-minute interview. The partner mumbled something vaguely apologetic about a "client emergency" and then proceeded to conduct the interview as if nothing happened. I politely explained that,

although the delay was not a problem, I did have another interview scheduled right after this one and thus would have to leave
after the allotted five minutes. To this the partner replied that five
minutes was not nearly enough to evaluate me, and that if I was
serious about working for his firm, I would have to stay and be late
to my next interview. I did not bother.

Another partner was famous for giving candidates the silent treatment. Literally. During a lateral interview with this particular partner, Jason was led into an office while the partner was on the
phone. As he silently greeted the partner and sat down, his interviewer continued the phone conversation without as much as even
acknowledging Jason's presence. After the phone call ended 10
minutes later, the partner turned to checking his e-mail, while Jason
continued to sit there. At this point, Jason decided to break the
silence and ask his interviewer a question, but the partner simply
ignored it, which is when Jason got up and started to walk out.
"Where are you going?" the partner asked. "We are not done here."
"Thank you for your time," Jason replied. "Our interview really
helped me make a decision about my future at this firm."

Unfortunately, arrogance among interviewers is not solely confined to
law firm partners. Associates can be just as bad.

After a callback interview with one of the firm's partners, I was
propelled into the office of one of the senior associates. The associate let out a big sigh and rolled her eyes when I was introduced.
Then, once the door was shut, she proceeded to give me the most
hostile interview of my life, sneering at my journal membership
and involvement in campus activities. After shredding my resume
to bits, she gave me a halfhearted pitch for the firm, unenthusiastically
listing benefits such as an in-house gym and "humane" billable-
hour requirements. As proof that the firm supposedly valued
"work-life balance," she mentioned that she was going on vacation
the next day. I didn't particularly care about her vacation plans.
But, trying to be polite, I said, "How nice. Where are you going?"
She reacted as though I had just asked for her Social Security number, credit score, and blood type. She shot me a suspicious glare,
and backed her chair away a foot or so. "Why do you need to
know that?" "I don't know," I said, confused. "I was just asking."
"Well I'm just going with my husband somewhere, okay?"

Hopefully, these stories will not be representative of your own interviewing experience. In most cases, legal interviews are fairly uneventful,
and interviewers are courteous and polite. But it is important to be prepared for the unexpected and to know in advance how you can deal with
these sticky situations without risking your own reputation or an offer.

Do Not Overreact

If you do not have the luxury of walking out, or if you prefer to hold off on making a decision until after receiving an offer, resist the temptation to walk out, be rude back, or report the interviewer's bad behavior. Although these actions may give you instant gratification, they can also jeopardize your chances of an offer and even tarnish your own reputation.

Payton, a second-year law student, lost an opportunity to interview in the fall of her 2L year because she was rude to her interviewer. Although it was the interviewer who triggered Payton's reaction by calling her law school performance "inadequate," the law school career services still decided to discipline her for her rude behavior. Payton was barred from interviewing on-campus for the rest of the year. To add insult to injury, her name made it onto several discussion boards, making it more difficult for her to land interviews on her own.

Remember to keep your cool. Keep in mind that an interviewer who is making arrogant remarks in your presence may be simply testing your reaction to see if you can withstand the pressure of the job.

Mark, who interviewed for a prestigious government position, can attest to that. Two of Mark's interviewers were extremely rude and obnoxious. They ignored him, talked amongst themselves, lambasted his resume and lack of experience, and gave him negative feedback about his interview performance. Of course, Mark could have simply walked out of the interview. But this was his dream job, and he had waited several years to get an interview, so he withstood the attacks. He was offered the job, and he soon discovered the reason for the interviewers' behavior: The position involved a lot of pressure from outside sources, and it was critical for the candidate to be able to keep his or her cool at all times. So the interviewers were pushing Mark's buttons in order to find out whether he was a good fit for this position. In the end, Mark's ability to recognize that he should not react negatively to the interviewers' behavior was what helped him get the job of his dreams.

Also keep in mind that you may have simply misunderstood the interviewer by mistaking his or her behavior for rudeness. As one student will tell you, this mistake can cost you dearly.

> Eric was interviewing on campus during his 2L year at a third-tier school. Eric had high grades, but he was really concerned about the interviewers' potential negative perception of his lower-ranked school. So the only reaction that came to Eric when his interviewer did not show up to his scheduled interview was anger. It was this anger that prompted Eric to write a long, bitter letter to the interviewer. The letter scolded the potential employer for ignoring scheduled interviews simply because they were at a lower-ranked school. As it turned out, there was a simple computer error, and the interviewer was misinformed about the time of his first interview that day. He would have gladly rescheduled if it were not for Eric's rude letter. Eric's reaction to this simple misunderstanding precluded him from working for this firm.

Finally, do not hastily pass judgment on the interviewer's firm. Most legal employers have at least one bad apple among them, and this is not necessarily representative of the employer as a whole. Some interviewers behave this way simply because they are having a stressful day at work. Some bad apples are not so bad once you get to know them.

> Jesse was interviewed by a partner who was rude, curt, and gave him the silent treatment during an interview. The partner just did not know how to be a good interviewer. When Jesse ended up working with this partner later on, he discovered she actually was a nice person and a great boss.

So remember to give the firm and the interviewer the benefit of a doubt.

Ask Questions

When it comes to rude questions, the substance of your answer does not matter as much as your reaction. The best thing you can do is stay calm, consider your response, and think twice before saying anything at all. Then try to give your best answer, using the same tone and exhibiting the same demeanor you would use answering a question in a moot court competition—respectful and dispassionate. Your answers to arrogant questions should be unemotional, concise, and on point. Likewise, if you are given the silent treatment, take initiative by asking questions; or smile or nod, and wait politely for the silence to end.

Because arrogant interviewers can make it difficult for you to ascertain the quality of the workplace, you need to refocus their attention by asking questions about the firm. These questions can help you determine the true culture and philosophy of the firm. Consider asking any of the following: "What does the firm expect from new lawyers?" "What interactions do associates have with partners?" "What qualities do you value the most in the people you hire?" and "How can a young lawyer succeed at your firm?" Questions such as these can help you gain insights into the firm's politics and culture. If, however, after the interview, you are still concerned about working at the firm, ask for an opportunity to meet other attorneys before making your decision. You may discover that, unlike your interviewer, the other attorneys at the firm are friendly and courteous.

Remember, you are seeking a long-term professional opportunity. Although it may feel poetic to act offended and walk out in the middle of an interview, this may not be in your best interest, professionally speaking. Always remember that this could be the firm or organization where you end up spending most of your professional career. Try to attribute any obnoxious behavior to stress, shyness, a complete lack of a personal life, or a difficult work-life balance. After all, if you need to vent, you can always contribute to Abovethelaw.com and expose your "interview from hell" story there.

QuickReview

✓ When faced with an arrogant interviewer, think first and react later.

✓ Always think carefully about what you are going to say and the likely consequences of your words.

✓ Make sure you do not mistake an innocent question or behavior for rudeness.

✓ Note that some interviewers (especially those in Big Law firms) use rudeness to test your sensibilities and your ability to withstand pressure.

✓ Being rude back to your interviewer can damage your reputation in the legal community.

✓ Do not be too quick to judge your interviewer based on one comment, remark, or incident, and do not form an opinion about the employer based on one brief encounter.

Chapter 17

LUNCH, DINNER, AND RETREAT INTERVIEWS

Most candidates attend a number of interview lunches, which are often a part of callback and lateral interviews. Although lunch interviews are more common, breakfast, dinner, and cocktail interviews are not unheard of. The important thing to remember here is not to treat these interviews casually. Even when your interviewers are the same age as or younger than you, maintain professionalism and decorum in your conversation, and never let your guard down.

Act Professional

A growing numbers of firms invite candidates for breakfast, lunch, or dinner interviews. The idea behind these interviews is for attorneys to get to know the candidates and to share insights about the firm. Because these interviews seem so relaxing, they often give young lawyers an unusual surge of confidence. Nevertheless, certain basic rules of conduct apply.

Do not do or say anything foolish (getting drunk or hitting on someone are good examples). Do not act like this is the first all-expense-paid fancy dinner you have ever attended, even if it is. Do not overeat, and shy away from the most expensive items on the menu. Additionally, do not treat dinner interviews as a date or a social call.

During his dinner interview, Luke, a 3L, tried unsuccessfully to hit on his female interviewer. Upon discovering she was not interested, Luke switched to flirting with some women at a nearby table. Proudly proclaiming himself to be a "corporate lawyer," he bought shots for the ladies and gulped down several drinks. He spent the remainder of the firm dinner making out with his new "date," right in front of his interviewers.

It is easy to relax, get too casual, and feel at the top of your game when someone is paying for your meal at a nice restaurant and you have had a few drinks. Do not forget that you are attending a job interview! The firm is providing you with a free dinner, not with a complimentary dating service.

Never Let Your Guard Down

Typically, the interviewers attending these events are junior to mid-level associates. When no one else is available, or when you share a similar background with one of the attorneys, your interviewers may be more senior. Conversations during these interviews are usually informal, convivial, and not necessarily confined to any particular topic. This is your chance to ask questions about the firm's culture and work environment. But do not let your guard down!

> Jeff thought it was a good idea to becomes buddies with his lunch interviewers. He ordered martinis and told the interviewers about his outlook on firm life. Basically, he wanted to land a job where he could work as little as possible. Although the interviewers understood Jeff's desire to not work hard and even found his remarks amusing, as his potential supervisors they were not impressed. They knew that, upon joining the firm, Jeff would likely dodge assignments, leaving them to pick up the slack. So they communicated these concerns to the recruiting manager, who promptly sent Jeff a rejection letter.

Never forget: This is still very much an interview. Avoid doing or saying anything you would not do or say at a more traditional interview. Do not confide in your interviewers or share negative feelings about any topic.

> Andrey interviewed with a litigation boutique known for conducting informal callback interviews. After the first round of interviews, Andrey was invited for beer and pizza at the partner's house. It went so well that Andrey was then asked to continue the night with scotch and poker at the firm's office. Andrey, who was an avid poker player, was feeling very relaxed at this point. Excited about winning, he began making snotty remarks to his new poker buddies, at one point saying, "He really put his d*** on the table," regarding one interviewer's strong bet. Not surprisingly, Andrey never heard from the firm again.

Finally, do not ask associates any questions you would not be comfortable asking the partners. The questions will get answered, but it might come at a price. Furthermore, do not be too casual, no matter how junior the interviewers or how informal the setting.

Kathy asked the associate interviewing her whether the partner she saw earlier that morning was "*really* nice," or whether he was acting nice because of the interview. Lenny asked his interviewers how he could justify to his family working for a firm that represents controversial clients. Keith spent the entire interview talking about his newborn baby, and then asked whether he could telecommute to work. None of these people received offers.

What to Order?

During interviews, the person paying should order first. This sets the tone for the spending behavior and your menu. Take your cues from the interviewers. Firms usually limit the budget for lunch interviews, so it is good to be mindful and not order too much. This may be difficult to do, especially if the interviewers invite you to order first. What you can do, however, is pick a moderately priced entrée and hold off on ordering appetizers. If your interviewers decide to order appetizers, you can then say something such as, "Actually, may I have a soup before my entrée as well? It sounds delicious." Or you can forgo the formalities and order a soup or an appetizer anyway. Even if you are the only person who orders an appetizer before your entrée, this move alone will not cost you an offer. Just do not order an appetizer for everyone to share—your interviewers will not take it well, especially because they are paying for your meal.

Most interviewers do not care what you order, as long as you do not blow the budget completely and do not order alcohol without their invitation. Some interviewers, however, try to infer something about you as a person from your luncheon selections.

Joseph once attended a lunch interview at a trendy midtown spot in Manhattan, frequented mostly by people with expense accounts. The interviewer, a junior associate at a large New York firm, seemed determined to ignore Joseph while she was preoccupied with her BlackBerry. After a few minutes, she finally looked up and suggested they order appetizers. She ordered a seafood appetizer that was sprinkled with caviar. He picked a $12 lobster roll, which was studded with a few pieces of real lobster. The associate quickly reprimanded Joseph for ordering lobster at an interview: "Although you won't lose any points with me, other people could think it's inappropriate." The interview was getting awkward, so Joseph made an attempt at humor: "I'm sorry. Can I make it up to you by ordering a bottle of the best champagne in the house?" He made her laugh, thus easing the tension.

Everything is relative, and food choices and attempts at humor are no exception. If in doubt, let the interviewer be your guide. In case you are curious, Joseph did not order champagne, and he did receive an offer from the firm. Generally, though, you can order almost anything on the menu without risking losing a potential offer. Just stay away from lobster, caviar, pricy wines, and similar delicacies, unless your interviewers expressly invite you to indulge.

Finally, only order desserts if your interviewers insist you do so. Most of the time, interviewers will politely ask you about dessert or coffee while secretly hoping you will decline. This is because desserts make long interviews even longer, and interviewers are usually eager to return to work by this time. Therefore, unless someone at the table actually orders dessert or coffee, refrain from ordering them. The interviewers' schedules may be more relaxed during dinner, but again, watch for cues.

Table Manners

It is amazing how many candidates lack basic table manners. We have seen interviewees who pick their teeth, eat with their bare hands, or put their elbows on the dining table. Some also slurp, talk with their mouths full, and munch their food loudly during interviews. If you were raised in a family in which proper table manners were not a priority, pay special attention to how you eat and behave. Do not gulp down your entrée, because eating quickly looks unattractive. When ordering, remember that foods that you can eat with a fork and knife tend to be safer than foods such as burgers and ribs. If you reach into the bread basket, go ahead and cut or break off a piece of bread, but never place the piece you took back into the basket.

> During her lunch interview, Amanda took the piece of bread from the basket, buttered it, took a bite, and put the same piece back in the basket. The first interviewer immediately picked up a BlackBerry and started typing frantically. The second interviewer then excused himself as he was checking his BlackBerry, explaining he had an urgent client e-mail. What he was actually reading was an e-mail from the first interviewer, with the subject line "Bread," and the question "Did she just do that?" in the body of the text.

Furthermore, never criticize your interviewers' choice of a restaurant: A lunch interview is not about enjoying the cuisine. There is absolutely no room for grimacing, complaining, or sighing about the food or restaurant. Most of the time, you will be able to find a few vegetarian, kosher, or non-ethnic entrees on any restaurant menu. The only thing you will accomplish by telling your interviewers you dislike their choice of a restaurant is making them feel bad. And their negative feelings, whether intentionally or not, may later affect their impressions about your candidacy and cost you an offer. For the same reason, if you can help it, try not to order a dish that indicates a subtle critique of the restaurant selection. Although ordering chicken in a seafood restaurant will not cost you an offer, it may suggest to your interviewers that you disapprove of their choice.

> Mike, an Alabama native, found himself at a lunch interview that specialized in soul food. Apparently, his D.C. interviewers went to great lengths to find a restaurant that would make Mike feel at home. Mike actually preferred Japanese cuisine, as soul food was definitely not a novelty for him. But he bit his tongue and thanked the interviewers profusely for being so considerate. His positive attitude did not go unnoticed.

Basic Etiquette

Here are some useful etiquette tips for your meal interviews:

1. After sitting down, place the napkin on your lap or allow the server to place it for you.

2. Your bread and salad plates are always on your left, and your drinking glass is on your right. Utensils start from the outside in, and the dessert fork is by the dessert plate. Placing your fork and knife side by side across your plate signals to your server that you are finished.

3. Order easy-to-eat items. There is no graceful way to eat barbequed ribs. If you order fish, you may want to make sure it does not have any bones. Stay away from soups if you tend to slurp.

4. Never ask the server to customize your order.

5. Pass bread, appetizers, and other items to the person on your right.

6. Do not reach for something across the table. Always ask the person nearest you to pass it.

7. If someone asks you to pass the salt, pass both salt and pepper.

8. If soup is served, hold the spoon away from you to help stop the drips. Sip from the side of the spoon and do so quietly. To get the last little bit of soup, tilt the bowl away from you. When you are finished, leave the spoon in the bowl.

9. When someone passes you the butter, cut a small piece, place it on your bread plate, and pass the butter to the person on your right. Tear off a small piece of bread to butter.

10. Always thank your companions for the meal, even though the firm is paying.

11. Additionally, remember to thank your interviewers for their time. They are spending precious, otherwise-billable time to take you out and tell you about the firm. Do not assume they are there because they have nothing better to do, or because they want a free meal. Eating takeout while billing time allows them to go home early, and it surely beats having a two-hour lunch with a stranger. To them, this is a time commitment, not a treat.

Alcohol

Generally, do not drink unless you are encouraged to. Never drink during lunch interviews, even if others are drinking. Order a drink (or two, depending on what your limit is) during firm retreats or receptions, but drink in moderation. You have probably heard about "Aquagirl"—a student who got so drunk at a firm event that she took off her clothes, handed them to a partner, and jumped into the Hudson River. She had to be fished out of the river by the Coast Guard while the firm's partners, associates, clients, and summer associates watched. In another recent scandal, two female summer associates were fired after getting drunk and making out with each other at a firm event.

Although your interviewers may be trying to drink each other under the table, do not follow in their footsteps. Likewise, do not enroll in shot-drinking competitions at these events. Your interviewers already have jobs and do not care about getting drunk, passing out under the table, or making fools out of themselves. But when they sober up, they will remember what you did. Trust us, you do not want to be known as "that guy/gal who did all those shots" at the firm event. If you must drink, drink wine rather than hard liquor, and never drink more than two glasses.

Finally, do not drink on an empty stomach. By the time you are invited to have a drink, you have likely spent most of the day in interviews and not eaten much. Eat something before you drink. The last thing you want is to get drunk or tired before the evening even begins. Pay no attention to your interviewers' drinking habits. They already have jobs, and likely several years of practice in a profession known for substance abuse. You are not yet in the same league, so take it easy.

Chase got so hammered during a dinner interview that he started hitting on the hiring partner's wife. He told her she was a hottie and asked for her phone number. He then threw up all over the hiring partner. Finally, Chase passed out in the partner's wife's lap. Of course, there was no chance he would receive an offer after that. Even worse, this incident followed him around for many years afterward.

At Firm Retreats, Be a Team Player

An invitation to a firm retreat is the latest experiment some firms are trying out as a part of their recruiting efforts. Despite their obvious curb appeal, firm retreats are basically day- or week-long interviews, so all the usual interview rules apply.

Try to have a good time, but do not treat a retreat as a vacation. Be a good sport; when invited to participate in team-building exercises or competitive activities, do it with a smile. The most important aspect of such exercises is not your performance, but your ability to get along well with others. If you happen to lose, lose gracefully. Likewise, if your interviewers push your buttons, never push back.

Make an effort to spend most of your waking moments with your interviewers. It may be tempting to check into the 24-hour spa on the premises or to sign up for day-long golf lessons, but remember—you are there on a firm's dime, interviewing for a job. The firm expects you to put in a lot of face time and to be available during exercises, meetings, and other events. Socializing can help you improve your chances, so get to know your future colleagues and learn more about the firm.

A meal or retreat interview should be an enjoyable experience for both you and your interviewers. It should also give you an opportunity to learn more about the firm and the interviewers while letting them get to know more about you. Remember not to say or do anything during these interviews you would not say or do during regular interviews. Although your interviewers may appear friendly and casual, they are carefully watching your every move. Enjoy these events and try to have fun, but act professionally.

QuickReview

✓ Be on your best behavior during informal interviews and never let your guard down.

✓ Do not volunteer any information you would not divulge during a regular interview.

✓ Do not order anything too expensive or exotic.

✓ Do not drink alcohol unless you are invited to.

✓ Follow your interviewers' lead in ordering appetizers and desserts.

✓ Watch your table manners and avoid messy foods.

✓ Do not criticize the interviewers' restaurant choice.

✓ Do not treat these interviews as an opportunity to get too familiar, casual, or flirtatious.

Part IV

❦

Interview Scenarios Throughout Your Career

Chapter 18

Big Firms vs. Small Firms

ᏄᎳᎪᏃ

This chapter addresses the major differences between interviewing at big and small firms. But be aware that there are many variations in interviewing styles at different firms, and many firms, especially medium-sized firms, which are not discussed here, may fall at any spot on the spectrum. This chapter provides general advice for interviewing at larger (200-plus attorneys) and smaller (50 or less attorneys) firms. After reading this chapter, review Chapter 3 and conduct firm-specific research to determine which approach to take.

Major Differences

Interviews with large firms are very predictable. In a good economy, large firms are not afraid to spend money on on-campus interviews. They often try to impress candidates by printing marketing brochures, offering refreshments to the students, and interviewing in teams of two. Callback interviews at large firms are almost always on schedule, and even if someone cancels or is running late, the recruiter will take care of the issue so quickly, you will not even notice.

Interviews with small firms are less predictable, and you are subject to much more scrutiny. Furthermore, unlike large firms, small firms may not care as much about making their interviewees too comfortable. Rather, their goal is to ensure that the candidate's personality fits well within the firm. As a result, small firms often conduct interviews in a more thorough and unusual way that helps them decide whether a candidate will make a great attorney, and whether he or she possesses the required social skills to survive in the intimate environment of a small firm.

As a 1L, Adam attended a callback interview at a small New Orleans firm. This was his first callback interview; not knowing what to expect, he was prepared for anything—

anything, that is, except the eight partners and one senior associate who met him in a windowless conference room, all jump-
ing up to say hello and extending their hands the moment he
came in. Although he was surprised, Adam was back on his feet
a few seconds later, saying hi to everyone at once. Backed against
the wall, he had nowhere to go but around the room. And so
he did, shaking each of their hands in turn in a clockwise direction. He later learned he was the only candidate that day who
passed the "back against the wall" test and received an offer.

Big Firm, Big Budget

Money is more of an issue for small firms than large firms. BigLaw
firms interview in bulk, and they do not hesitate to spend money on the
interviewees—again, sometimes in bulk.

During one callback interview with a large New York
firm, Jason was invited for a breakfast with a couple of
associates the morning before the interview. At first, he
thought this was a nice touch. When he arrived there, however,
he was surprised to find out that the firm had also invited 26
other candidates to the same breakfast. They were joined by a
few associates from the firm, none of whom knew anything about
the candidates. Breakfast was pre-ordered, and the whole af-
fair felt like a Costco approach to shopping for associates—buy
'em in bulk and save big. This is not to say this firm would not be
a good place to work.

At large firms, the interviewing process runs like a well-oiled machine.
Every candidate interviewing at big firms gets to stay in a nice hotel if he is
from out-of-town; meets at least four to six attorneys; dines at an expensive restaurant on the firm's dime; and receives congratulatory e-mails and
follow-up phone calls from his interviewers when he gets an offer. There
are urban legends about candidates receiving extra-special attention from
firms that really wanted to hire them.

One candidate, who was African-American, the editor-
in-chief of the law review, at the top of his class, and at a top
law school, was supposedly flown to a callback on a private
jet! This firm desperately needed to hire more minority attorneys.
This student also happened to have excellent credentials, so the
firm decided to go the extra mile. In case you are wondering, he
didn't take the offer. He was very tempted, but he chose to join a
smaller firm instead so he could spend more time with his family.

Most candidates do not receive special treatment above and beyond that of the rest of the talent pool. Most large firms have a preset budget for each callback interview and they stick to it. You will stay at a nice hotel and eat a nice lunch on the firm's dime, but usually no private jets or first-class tickets are involved.

Things not to do when interviewing at large firms

You don't have to worry as much about formalities when interviewing with large firms. Once you land a callback, your chances of getting an offer from a big firm are fairly good. Some BigLaw recruiters estimate that they make offers to 50 to 75 percent of the candidates invited for callbacks. And for firms that engage in more careful screening process, this percentage is even higher. Still, there are plenty of ways to screw up a Big Law interview.

During her lunch interview, Carrie—apparently feeling a touch overconfident that she'd already clinched an offer—told the interviewer about her prior summer associate experience. The attorneys routinely took her out to lunches in an effort to get to know her—two-hour lunches that usually included appetizers and desserts and made her sleepy. So, she revealed to her interviewer, she used to shut her office door and take afternoon naps. Not something you want to say to a person who is thinking about hiring you!

We mentioned before that large firms hire in bulk. As a result of this, you do not need to worry as much about writing a detailed thank-you letter. With large firms, it is actually better to send it via e-mail to ensure it gets there on time. To maintain the appearance of formality, you can include the requisite introduction, body, and conclusion paragraphs, with your first and last name at the bottom. You may also send it as an e-mail attachment, which means you are following proper formalities while also ensuring speedy delivery. E-mail is probably best, and one or two professional-sounding sentences are sufficient. Write it as soon as possible after the interview.

With big firms, you may often get an offer before you have a chance to write your thank-you letter. Some large firms believe that giving an offer on the spot will increase the likelihood that you will accept. They may even put a nice spin on it by saying something along these lines: "Although we typically wait until Friday to meet with the hiring committee to discuss all of our candidates, everyone was so impressed with you that we decided there was no point in waiting." If this happens to you, congratulations! But do not feel too flattered. Most of the time, this is just a hedging strategy designed to increase acceptance rates. Do not feel pressured or obligated to accept an offer without taking the opportunity to look around first. Assuming that the economy is healthy and there aren't too many other acceptances, the offer will still be there after you have had a chance to interview with other employers.

Smaller Firm, Smaller Budget

In contrast, small firms must carefully handpick their candidates before bringing them in. The reason for this is simple: Smaller firms do not have the resources necessary to bring in many people to interview. Callback interviews are expensive and time-consuming. As a result, small firms screen their candidates very carefully prior to bringing them in. Additionally, students often must travel to the interviews at small firms on their own dime. They are also less likely to be taken out for a nice free lunch.

At some small firms, you may go through three to four rounds of interviews and end up meeting every attorney in the firm. These firms employ a thorough evaluation process because they view personality fit as crucial. Meanwhile, at other small firms, you may not even have a callback; you may receive an offer after an on-campus or phone interview, or—if you are really lucky—one solely based on your resume.

After receiving an offer from a small firm, consider asking for an opportunity to visit the firm again to help you make a more informed decision. Additionally, never accept on the spot or you will forgo an opportunity to negotiate. Unlike big firms, small firms are more flexible when it comes to negotiating such things as moving expenses, compensation, bonuses, and vacation time. Ask for what is reasonable, and be prepared to go through several rounds of negotiations before settling on the final package. And, of course, review Chapter 29 to help you prepare.

Things not to do when interviewing at small firms

Lawyers in small firms are more cautious and conservative when it comes to hiring. They handpick candidates who can easily adapt to various settings, who are confident, and who have great personalities. They will not risk hiring a candidate who may not fit in well, who is not confident enough to handle added responsibility, or who is not absolutely certain he or she wants to practice the type of law the firm practices.

Small firms expect their candidates to be professional and very well-prepared. This means wearing a conservative dark suit; having extra copies of your resume, transcripts, and writing samples handy; listening without interrupting; and acting friendly (but not too casual). Small firms also usually care less about school rankings and credentials than larger firms do, and they may give a stronger preference to candidates who can emphasize relevant experience. Additionally, candidates who are humble and personable are more likely to get offers than those who brag about going to top-tier schools or being on the law review. Because personality and relevant experience are the key to acing small-firm interviews, put your best foot forward. Be professional without appearing too formal or dry. To minimize the risk of appearing arrogant, let your resume speak for itself when it comes to achievements, but proactively discuss relevant work projects. Focus on interests, hobbies, and your passion for the type of law the firm practices.

Interviewers at small firms expect formal, mailed thank-you letters. A handwritten note at the bottom of a typed thank-you letter is a welcome touch, provided you have good penmanship. This may be the one thing that will help convince the partners to choose you over other qualified candidates.

Finally, during small-firm interviews, do not discuss big firms, large corporate clients, huge class-action settlements, or your hopes of doing large-scale defense work or practicing international law. Small firms can be sensitive about the fact that they are small. Even when they tell you with pride that they refused to grow through mergers in order to preserve their unique culture, they do not want an indication that you have big-firm envy.

The differences between interviewing with big firms and small firms are telling. Large firms are corporate institutions, where constant recruiting and attrition are the cost of doing business. They expect a certain number of attorneys to pass through the firm and leave. On the other hand, although small firms are not immune to attrition, depending on their size and culture, they may feel that your addition to the firm will have a lasting impact on their work environment. Keep this in mind as you approach your interviews.

QuickReview

✓ Be especially mindful of the interviewing budget when dealing with smaller firms.

✓ Big firms interview in bulk and follow a standard, step-by-step interviewing process.

✓ With small firms, expect the unexpected and prepare to be flexible.

✓ Be conservative and personable when interviewing at small firms.

✓ Do not engage in "big-firm talk" while interviewing at small firms.

✓ Thank-you letters are a must for small firms. The ideal thank-you letter for a small firm is a formal typed letter with a handwritten note at the bottom.

✓ The ideal thank-you letter for a large firm is a formal e-mail or a letter sent as an attachment, sent as soon as possible after the interview.

✓ Never accept an offer on the spot.

Chapter 19

ON-CAMPUS INTERVIEWS

ⓔⓙⓧⓧⓔ

> During a somewhat dry on-campus interview that took place at the end of the day, a partner asked a 2L candidate what he thought about the interviewing process. The student turned the interview around with a witty answer. He pondered for a second and said, "On-campus interviewing is like speed-dating. There are many different suitors. Many are attractive. Some carry the promise of a second date, and some do not. Then, there are all these talks about needing to see other people." The partner was very pleased with this answer, and the candidate received a callback for thinking on his feet.

This speed-dating metaphor really sums up the key features of on-campus interviewing. Similar to dating, an on-campus interview involves getting to know someone in a very short time, convincing him or her that you are an attractive candidate, and sounding interesting enough for him or her to want to see you again.

Try to Stand Out

Even if you have never been to a speed-dating event, you probably know what it entails: Two people sit on different sides of a table and have a short amount of time to decide if they are compatible. Then they move on to new participants. On-campus interviews last only 20 minutes, and a typical interviewer meets 12 to 20 candidates a day. By the end of a long day on campus, interviewers often have a hard time putting together the names and faces of the students they met. In addition to demeanor, dress code, and bold moves, a key way to stand out during on-campus interviews is to be positive and upbeat, and to make a lasting first impression. Just as with speed dating, first impressions make all the difference.

Interview Structure

Unless your interviewer takes charge of the interview, it is your job to budget your time wisely. Ideally, you should spend the first 15 minutes talking about yourself and about your interviewer, and save the remaining five minutes for asking questions.

If you do not click with your interviewer, it may become difficult to maintain the right interview structure. During interviews filled with awkward silences, the interviewer may ask you, "So, what can I tell you about my firm?" This question is bad for at least three reasons: first, it does not help you sell yourself; second, the interviewer is not showing much interest in you; and third, if you start asking questions about the firm so early into the interview, you may run out of questions before it is over. Try to prevent this by being an engaging conversationalist, by listening carefully and following up, and by learning to fill awkward silences. If your interviewer asks if you have any questions early in the interview, go ahead and ask a few.

> In an inauspicious start to the interview, the interviewer asked Vanessa, "So, what can I tell you about the firm?" Startled, Vanessa asked, "Are you hiring litigators?" He said, "Yes—good ones. Are you good?" Vanessa floundered for a moment, but, deciding it was not the time to be modest, said, "I am! Let me tell you why...."

As you can see, telling a story, sharing similar experiences, or using the interviewer's answers to describe how you can excel at the firm are all excellent ways to bring the interview back to yourself. And always remember to interject a few selling points into the interview to help convince your interviewer that you are a strong candidate.

Just as importantly, do not ask questions about the firm prematurely on your own initiative. Try to find common ground with your interviewer by discussing other things besides your credentials. And if you are having a great time talking about the weather, baseball, law school, or whatever tickles your mutual fancy, continue doing so. That way, when the interview ends, your interviewer will feel as though the time flew by, and that there were still things that he or she wanted to talk about. You want to leave your interviewer with this feeling because he or she will then want to meet you again and give you a callback. Simply put, just as you would on a first date, you want to leave your interviewer wanting more.

Protocol

On-campus interviewing can be a stressful, fast-paced process. Various issues may arise. We deal with scheduling issues, inappropriate behavior, and arrogant interviewers elsewhere in this book. Here are several additional issues to keep in mind specifically during on-campus interviewing.

First, if you are running late or cannot make it to your interview, make sure to notify the employer or your career services as soon as possible so that they can make adjustments to the interviewer's schedule or give your slot to another student. Never miss an interview simply because you decided you have no interest in pursuing employment with the firm. Likewise, if you know ahead of time you have to miss an interview, try to find a classmate to take your slot.

Second, always be respectful and courteous, not only to your interviewers, but also to your classmates. Always arrive to the interview at least 10 minutes early to ensure you can find the room and take a deep breath before your interview begins. This way, you may even be rewarded with additional time if the interview before yours ends early. Being on time also ensures that your interview will not run over, and that your classmates will be able to keep their own interviewing schedules intact. This courtesy makes a good impression.

Third, always ask interviewers if they would like to take a short break before meeting with you. Although they will probably politely decline, they will appreciate the fact that you were courteous enough to acknowledge that they may not have had a chance to take a break for several hours.

Fourth, because interviews sometimes run longer than the allotted time period, you may end up in a situation in which you risk being late to your next interview if it is immediately following. Of course, you can avoid this by following the advice in Chapter 2, and by not scheduling back-to-back interviews. But if you cannot prevent it, knock on the door at your scheduled time, reminding the interviewer that it is your turn. If you do not get a response, knock again a few minutes later. Finally, knock for the third time after five minutes. Most of the time, the interviewer will at least acknowledge your presence at that point. If you receive no response after the third knock, try to wait as long as you can, and definitely do not make an issue out of it.

Fifth, if you have back-to-back interviews scheduled, and your first interview starts late, let your interviewer know right away that you might have to leave before he or she gets the chance to finish. This way, you will not only get to leave on time, but you will also give your interviewer a chance to budget his or her time accordingly.

Finally, keep in mind that the primary purpose of on-campus interviews is for potential employers to get to know you. This means that you don't have to limit yourself to talking solely about your qualifications; rather, you can talk about anything that would be of interest to your interviewer and help you connect on a human level. Just like being on a first date, it does not really matter what you talk about as long as both people are having a good time. And, just like being on a first date, there is only one major rule: Do not talk about the future. An interview is not the time to ask about your chances of making partner, what your compensation would be, or how offers are communicated. Take it slow and try to enjoy the process.

On-campus interviews are like no other. They are fast-paced and stressful. For employers, on-campus interviews are difficult because they must keep track of dozens or even hundreds of candidates. To navigate through this difficult process and to stand out, approach these interviews as you would speed dating. Impress each interviewer, find a way to connect with him or her on a personal level, be engaging, and ask thoughtful questions. Beyond that, remember to follow the standard interviewing protocol and be courteous. Once you master these skills, you will find on-campus interviews a rewarding and interesting experience.

QuickReview

✓ On-campus interviewers see dozens, even hundreds, of candidates daily and often have a hard time putting together names and faces.

✓ Do everything you can to stand out from the crowd.

✓ Try to find common ground with your interviewer and spend a few minutes chatting about something other than firms, interviews, and credentials.

✓ Make sure your interview is engaging, ask meaningful questions, and show genuine interest in your interviewer and the firm.

✓ Be very professional and courteous to others.

✓ If the interview does not start at the scheduled time, politely knock on the door; if you get no response, repeat this twice, two and five minutes later.

✓ Ask your interviewer if he or she would like to take a short break before starting your interview.

Chapter 20

CALLBACK INTERVIEWS AND THANK-YOU LETTERS

The rule of thumb used to be that once you got a callback, the offer was yours to lose. Not anymore. Employers no longer feel the need to hire every candidate who walks in the door. The constantly changing economy has triggered an increase in the competition for law jobs and allowed employers to be more selective. What does this mean for you? If an interviewer does not get the right vibe from you, the line may be drawn through your name instead of under it. Therefore, although your chances of getting an offer are still as good as anyone's (all things being equal), you should take callbacks very seriously and prepare carefully.

Do Not Let Your Guard Down

A typical callback involves meetings with several partners and anywhere from three to five associates of varying seniority. Shortly after your interview, all of your interviewers (including those who took you to lunch) will be asked to provide feedback regarding your candidacy. What you must know is that the partners' opinions carry greater weight. The partners are the ultimate decision-makers when it comes to job offers, and a very positive or a slightly negative encounter with a firm partner can easily make or break your offer. Meanwhile, assuming everyone else was impressed by you, a slightly negative comment in an associate's evaluation may not necessarily cost you an offer. But this does not mean you can ignore the associates, treat them poorly, or act informally during your interviews with them. Although associates are not the key decision-makers in your hiring, their votes are still important.

Never let your guard down, regardless of how young and friendly your interviewers are. Remember—they are there to evaluate you, not to make friends. They may act like your friends and encourage honest questions, but they will report to the hiring committee on your behavior and communication style. Do not ask for a lowdown on the firm, reveal personal

137

details of your life, pose controversial questions, or make inappropriate remarks.

> Becky was a bit too informal during her lunch interview. The interview was going well, and she was bonding with the junior associates interviewing her, until the subject of pets came up. Becky related a story about her family pet that liked to hump everything in sight. At first, the interviewers laughed. Encouraged and emboldened by their laughter, Becky proceeded to stand up from her chair and pantomime the pet's humping movements. This took place in an expensive, upscale restaurant. The result? A predictable rejection.

Finally, do not fall for the "you can ask me anything" line. Interviewers often encourage candid questions in an effort to discover a candidate's weak points. If your interviewer is feeding you this line, thank him or her and then politely ask a non-intrusive question about his or her work assignments, work-life balance, or relations with colleagues. Just make sure to phrase your questions in a positive way.

Do Not Overspend

Except during an economic downturn, many legal employers, including some government employers, will pay for some or all of your callback-related expenses. Callbacks with large national firms may even earn you a five-star treatment (reimbursements for airfare, nice accommodations, meals, and so on). Like most students, you may still consider ramen noodles and Chinese takeout to be major food groups. But your desire to treat yourself on a firm's dime should never lead to uncontrollable spending. Remember, even if you do not get or do not care to get an offer from this firm, recruiting coordinators from different firms talk amongst themselves and may even split your expenses if you interview with them on consecutive days. You probably will not get away with overspending.

> Mike did not get an offer precisely because of his unusual request for reimbursement after a callback. Although he did not overindulge on dinner or drinks, he happened to order (and charge to his room) a couple of adult movies at the hotel where he stayed. Naturally, the hiring partner did not think seeking reimbursement for those was "kosher." But this partner had an even stronger reason not to give Mike an offer— the same movie was ordered twice. The partner reasoned, "I don't want to hire someone who didn't get it the first time."

Other more "innocent" expenses may raise red flags, as well: $60 breakfasts, excessive cab receipts (for the taxis you and your friends took to go clubbing the night before your interview), three-course dinners for you and your significant other, and so on.

> Andrea, a 2L, was actually grilled on the phone by a recruiting manager, asking her how she could spend $80 on lunch. Although Andrea was eventually reimbursed for half of her expenses, the firm informed her via a formal letter that her claim for reimbursement was "beyond what is appropriate."

Most larger firms have relatively high reimbursement limits. They will probably pay for your dinner at an expensive restaurant, but they may frown if you also ask them to pay for a nice bottle of wine or your friend's dinner. Most of the time, you will know in advance what the firm's suggested budget is for these types of expenses. When in doubt, ask the firm's recruiting coordinator or your career counselors how much you should spend.

Send Thank-You Letters

A lawyer's time is valuable, so thanking your interviewers for taking the time to meet with you goes a long way. A good thank-you letter shows you really want the job, that you are willing to work hard, and that you take this opportunity seriously. It also helps you reconnect with your interviewers and receive better evaluations. Interviewers tell us that candidates who follow up with a thank-you note always leave the best impression. "But isn't that something people did 20 years ago?" you may ask. Yes. It worked then, and continues to work now. Although some career counselors tell candidates that thank-you letters are not required after callbacks, we believe it is interview malpractice not to send them. Additionally, for some employers—small firms, for example—thank-you letters are a must.

All other things being equal, if you do not send a thank-you letter, the employer will almost certainly give an offer to another candidate who did. Therefore, always send a thank-you letter after a callback to each of your interviewers and the recruiting coordinator; and do it as soon as possible. Interviewers usually fill out evaluations within hours or days of the interview, and a prompt letter can improve your evaluation.

To prepare for writing your thank-you letters, jot down your notes and impressions about your interviewers within a few hours after the callback. This will help you organize and personalize them. Additionally, because you may be overwhelmed by the number of people you met, these notes will help you remember the details of your interviews. Keep your thank-you letters concise—one to three short paragraphs, and never exceeding one page. Do not use time constraints as an excuse to send poorly written letters; interviewers often compare letters and even forward them to recruiting. Make sure your letters are free of typos and are not copycat versions of each other.

Finally, remember that you have two delivery options, e-mail and regular mail. Although regular mail is a more traditional and formal way, e-mail has its advantages: It is more likely to arrive while it can still have an impact on your evaluations; it is easy to send; and it saves time, paper, and stamps. It also makes it easy for your interviewer to respond to you or forward the message to his or her colleagues, explaining why you are a strong candidate. Although we strongly advocate the use of e-mail for thank-you letters, you are the best judge of whether this is the way to go. If you are interviewing with a very conservative employer, a judge, or a small firm, or if you can mail your letters on the day of the interview (so they are likely to reach your interviewer the next day), you may be better off mailing them. Alternatively, if you need prompt delivery while preserving the veneer of formality, you can e-mail a formal thank-you letter as an attachment. Regardless of which way you go, remember to send your letters soon after the interview.

In many ways, callback interviews are very similar to other legal interviews. So be sure to read other chapters in this book to help you prepare. Be mindful of the interviewers' decision-making power and put your best foot forward. Imagine your interviewer sitting across the table and asking, "So, why should I hire you?" Figure out how to convince your interviewers to do exactly that. Be very professional and polite with everyone, and never let your guard down when interviewing with junior attorneys. Be reasonable when seeking reimbursement. Finally, do not underestimate the importance of well-written, timely thank-you letters.

QuickReview

✓ Take callbacks seriously—you may be competing with more people than you think.

✓ Review other chapters in this book to help you prepare.

✓ Work extra hard to impress partners, but treat all interviewers with respect and professionalism.

✓ Never let your guard down.

✓ Do not fall for the "you can ask me anything" comment.

✓ Be conservative in your spending.

✓ Do not order extravagant meals or seek reimbursement for someone else's expenses.

✓ Jot down notes about your interviewers shortly after the interview.

✓ Write concise, personal, error-free thank-you letters and send them promptly.

Chapter 21

INTERVIEWING FOR 1Ls, 2Ls, AND 3Ls

Most larger firms hire law students through their summer programs. Additionally, some small and mid-sized firms hire students on a part-time basis during the law school year. You have a good chance of getting a job during your law school career regardless of your law school, seniority, and academics. You just may have to work harder, depending on how these factors play out. When preparing for your interviews, use the resources available through career services, including mock interviews and resume proofreading. This chapter addresses components that are unique to interviewing as a 1L, 2L, or 3L. In addition, be sure to review other chapters in this book to help hone your interviewing skills.

1L Interviews

Understand that your options are limited during your 1L interviewing season. This is because most legal employers prefer to fill their summer positions with 2Ls, who have more experience and are more likely to accept offers of permanent employment. Because 1Ls often use summer jobs as a stepping stone to more lucrative job opportunities next year, you must convince your interviewers of your sincere desire to do well and to return.

Location, location, location

Your ties to an area will significantly improve your chances of getting offers from employers in that area. Therefore, you should emphasize your desire to work in a certain location during your interviews. If interviewing with small firms, emphasize your desire to spend the next two summers in a firm where you hope to end up working for many years to come. If you have family or friends in the area, you may want to highlight your intent to move closer to them upon graduation. If you went to school there or lived there before, clearly articulate to your interviewers why you want to reside permanently in a certain geographical area. If, on the other hand, your only connection to the area is your desire to vacation there or your inability to get interviews anywhere else, you need to get creative. Never say, "I am interested in working here because your firm is here" or "I only got a callback from you." Instead, explain what special qualities make this employer your number-one choice and why you also want to be in this particular area.

> When Brett interviewed as a 1L, he told his Boston employers about growing up in metropolitan area and how he was looking to return to big-city life upon graduation. He then explained why Boston and this particular employer were his number-one choice. To his Memphis employers, Brett said this was a city where his grandmother was born, and he wanted to return to his roots. Finally, he related his desire to move his family to a small town in Alabama to his Alabama interviewers. He explained that he had no ties anywhere, and that he had researched the area and found it to be a perfect place to raise a family, grow old, and develop a professional reputation and close ties with the community. All of Brett's answers were sincere, and his efforts to secure a job were successful.

Be prepared

For many students, 1L year brings their first encounter with the interviewing process. Be prepared. Start by scheduling mock interviews with your school's career services. They will help you gain confidence and reveal the mistakes you would otherwise make during the actual interviews. Additionally, ask your career services whether there are any alumni willing to "mock" interview you. Interviews with law school alumni offer real-life perspective for how legal interviews work and give you yet another chance to brush up on your skills. Finally, recruit a friend or family member a day before your interview and practice with him or her. Give him or her a list of questions to ask you and seek critiques of your answers, demeanor, and preparation. You will discover that these exercises are most helpful in learning how to interview effectively.

Emphasize experience

During your 1L year, employers have limited information about your skills and abilities. As a result, be prepared to discuss other attributes that will help them conclude that you can pull your weight at the firm. Avoid complaining about the stress of your 1L year or about how difficult your job search is. By this time in their careers, your interviewers have seen the real stress, and they will not be sympathetic to your complaints. Instead, focus on your grades, volunteer work, extracurricular activities, writing experience, and research skills.

> Amber secured multiple offers by promoting her skills to her interviewers. She told them she was the only 1L in her school who had obtained both Lexis and Westlaw certification. She also emphasized her high grades on legal writing assignments and her experience as a school newspaper editor. Although her GPA was nowhere near perfect, she was able to convince the employers that her research and writing skills made her a strong candidate.

For small firms, which often lack sufficient resources to train junior attorneys, your ability to hit the ground running is especially important. During interviews with small firms, discuss your performance in classes relevant to the firm's practice, any positive feedback you received on your writing, and your people skills. If you have relevant undergraduate training or language skills, which may help the firm obtain new clients or give you more responsibility, point them out, as well.

Seek alternative summer jobs

If you are unsuccessful in receiving firm interviews, remember that you still have firm internships, government positions, research assistantships, nonprofit, pro bono, and judicial internships open to you. Also keep in mind solo practitioners, who often hire law students on an hourly basis during the summer. And realize that your 1L summer is a good time to explore workplaces you may want to join eventually but cannot afford initially because of student loans. This is a great time to ascertain what it would be like to be an assistant district attorney, a general counsel for an NGO, an in-house lawyer for a small tech company, a junior executive in the entertainment industry, or a lawyer in a four-person boutique.

Although these jobs do not pay much, if anything, they will offer great experience and provide you with a solid resume booster for your interviews next year. When interviewing for government positions, remember to review Chapters 22 and 23. Also be prepared to discuss law school classes, legal subjects, and famous cases, because questions on these topics are more common during these types of interviews.

2L Interviews

Your interviews as a newly minted 2L can significantly shape the beginning of your legal career by bringing you closer to a permanent job offer. Most 2Ls employed as summer associates receive offers to join their respective firms after graduation, and a large number of these offers are accepted. As a 2L, your job is not simply to get a job but also to get to know the employers in order to decide whether you want to work with them after graduation.

Geography

The fall of your 2L year is a good time to seriously consider where you want to be for the next few years. Depending on your law school, your GPA, and the economy, you may have fewer or more choices available. Either way, you need to decide where you can see yourself living, and where you cannot.

Employers can be equally concerned with geography, especially small firms and firms in smaller communities. Because of this, your ties to a certain area (or lack thereof) can make or break your candidacy. If you interview in Seattle because you grew up there and your entire family lives there, you will score major points with your interviewers. Meanwhile, avoid tenuous explanations that offer little or no evidentiary proof of a genuine commitment—for example, you like to hike, you enjoy the weather, or you always wanted to live on the West Coast. What if, after six months of non-stop rain, you decide you have had enough hiking and leave for Southern California? In that case, you may not be a good investment for the firm.

Christian's job search was unsuccessful because he could not explain why he wanted to be in Miami. He grew up and spent most of his life in New Jersey. At some point (likely during a spring break), he discovered Miami and decided he did not want to live anywhere else. As a 2L, he signed up to interview only with Miami firms. He sent out tons of resumes and even landed a few callbacks, but after he was asked "Why Miami?" each time, the interview effectively ended. He had no ties to the area and could not come up with a reason better than he simply loved the city.

You can see why it is important to consider all the reasons you want to be in a particular location. Even if do not have any ties to an area, you can at least tell the interviewer why you like it. Orient your explanation to the future and point out all the reasons why you are likely to stay there. For instance: "I have a family, and I know that San Diego is a very family-friendly city, offers a lot of activities for kids, has great schools, and is on the ocean, which is very important to my family because we sail." Naturally, your reasons can vary, and family does not have to be one of them. Just make sure your explanation is realistic and genuine, and does not suggest you are simply looking for some summer fun.

1L summer job

Another important aspect of your 2L interview is what you did the previous summer. Students often agonize about their efforts to secure a 1L summer job. But the truth is, your employers could probably care less about what you did as a 1L, as long as you had a law-related job and were committed to working hard. During the interviews, explain what your job entailed, what you learned, and why your experience convinced you to interview with this particular employer. Be prepared to explain why you are not going back to your 1L employer. When interviewing with small firms, which seek lawyers who can handle responsibility early on, be sure to emphasize how your 1L job taught you to take initiative and to work under pressure.

Practice areas

The type of law you want to practice after graduation becomes an important interview topic during your 2L year. This is something you must consider in tandem with your geographical preferences and long-term career goals. When you evaluate these factors, ask yourself where your potential clients would be located. The answer to this may be simple if your desired specialty is project finance (New York, D.C., and Houston) or entertainment law (Miami and L.A.). Other specialties may not be as easy to pinpoint geographically. Additionally, know that just because a firm lists a specialty or a practice group on their Website, it does not mean that the firm has significant work in or hires associates for that department.

Look up individual lawyers, research what they do, try to find out which cases they work on. Most importantly, do not limit your options unnecessarily by seeking to interview only with employers in a narrow field. Most law students have preconceived ideas about what they want to do upon graduation, but these ideas often stem from misinformation. Do not think you will join a firm and immediately specialize in international law, construction law, entertainment law, oil and gas, or international arbitrations. Most likely, unless you join a small specialized practice, you will do your share of due diligence or document review and research assignments. What you will end up specializing in a few years down the road will depend in large part on your firm, your mentors, and the clients' needs, and only in small part on your preferences.

Although it is unnecessary to commit to a narrow specialty during your interviews with larger firms, you will score major points with the employers if you tell them that you are leaning toward a certain practice area. (See Chapter 3 for a discussion of the two most common practice areas in larger firms, transactional and litigation.) Your interviews will also be more productive if you offer flexibility to your employers. Instead of insisting on working in some fancy area of law that exists only in law books, you may want to mention your general preferences, indicate interest in more than one area, and emphasize your flexibility.

When interviewing with small firms, discussing practice areas gets trickier. On the one hand, you must convince them in your versatility and ability to work on a variety of cases. On the other hand, you must convey your commitment and strong desire to do precisely the type of work the attorneys handle. You can master this task by telling your interviewers that you have a strong interest in their practice area, and by adding that you are also flexible and eager to meet the firm's needs.

Summer splits

Now is the time to decide whether you want to split your summer between two employers. There are good reasons to consider summer splits. Splitting your summer between different firms or cities will give you a glimpse of what it would be like in two very different places. It may also give you more options to consider. Moreover, you can earn significantly more by splitting the summer because you will probably work longer. Finally, working more during the summer means you will obtain more legal experience and skills.

Just remember not to ask about summer splits during your initial interviews. Generally, summer splits are disfavored (especially at larger firms) because they increase the risk that you will not accept an offer of permanent employment. But a number of legal markets—for example, the South and parts of the Midwest—still allow or even encourage summer splits.

Rely on career counselors

Most law students find something to gripe about with respect to career services. But remember, they are not there to get you a job; they are there to *help* you get one. Career services can provide you with information, experienced advice, mock interviews, and resume proofreading. Prior to your 2L interviewing season, it is wise to schedule a time to speak with your career counselors. Tell them about your goals, expectations, and academics. Do not expect them to set your world on fire, but take their advice to heart.

The best career services will try to get as many employers on campus as possible and to give you a lot of information about what these employers generally seek. But remember that their ability to attract employers on campus largely depends on your law school's rank. For Harvard, it is not that difficult; for a newly accredited Midwestern school in a smaller legal market, it may be nearly impossible. You should not discredit help from your career counselors because you don't think they are doing enough. It is your job to be proactive.

3L Interviews

Whether you are interviewing because you did not like your 2L firm, because you want to move, or because you did not get an offer, the process will be very different from last year's. Firms usually treat 3L interviewees as lateral candidates, so be sure to read Chapter 24 to help you prepare.

Why firms hire 3Ls

Small firms often interview 3Ls shortly before or soon after graduation. Most larger firms interview a small number of 3Ls in the fall. These firms hire 3Ls because (1) they cannot afford to hire through summer programs; (2) they still have a few spots open at a particular practice group; (3) they hope to lure outstanding candidates away from other firms; or (4) they anticipate expanding. If you know why the firm is considering you, you can increase your chances of receiving an offer by emphasizing that reason to your interviewer.

This is how Kendra was able to secure a job in a very competitive legal market. After her 2L summer in New York, she decided to relocate to a small town that only had a few large firms, and even those hired exclusively from their summer programs. Despite sending resumes to every firm in town, she only received one interview. Because this was her only chance to relocate to this town, Kendra did a great deal of homework before her interview. She discovered that the firm recently brought in a securities litigation partner and was looking to expand its securities presence in the area. During the interview, Kendra emphasized her interest in securities litigation, which helped her land the job.

Explain your reasons for interviewing

First and foremost, be prepared to discuss your reasons for interviewing as a 3L. If you did not have a legal job during the summer, come up with a good explanation. Never say you could not get a job or that you wanted a break. Offer good reasons for not having a paying job during your 2L summer (the economic downturn, a sick relative, summer school, and so on) or explain what you did to make up for lack of this experience (an externship or volunteer work, for example).

Only give positive reports about your 2L employer. Never badmouth the old firm in efforts to justify your desire to move or to "flatter" your interviewers by showing you like them more. Stay positive, say a few good things about your old employer, and only then explain your reasons for interviewing. Family needs, a desire to change practice areas or firm size, and a wish to relocate are all good reasons for interviewing as a 3L. You can say something along these lines: "I had a wonderful time at firm X and learned a great deal. I appreciated the mentorship of the attorneys and how approachable they were. Unfortunately, I discovered I was really interested in practice area Y, which firm X doesn't practice. That's why I am particularly interested in your firm."

Assuming you have an offer from your 2L employer, volunteer that information early in the interview. Although they may not ask you directly whether you have an offer (more likely, they will), it is on their mind. If you did not receive an offer from your 2L employer, you should plan your strategy for interviewing as a 3L very carefully. You must be scrupulously honest with your interviewers; any attempts to mislead them will likely backfire. But do not volunteer negative information unless and until you are asked.

If you are asked, make sure you have a good explanation for not getting an offer. For example, your firm may hire a large summer associate class every year but make only two offers at the end of the summer. Or your employer may have decided to make fewer offers because it anticipates a slowdown. Or your firm may have felt you would be a flight risk because of your lack of ties to the area. You may be one of many summer associates who did not receive an offer, which means the economy—and not your inappropriate behavior—may be to blame. If your reason is unrelated to a deficient work product or poor behavior, it will be easier to convince your interviewers to hire you. You can also see if any attorneys at your old firm would be willing to serve as a reference and hopefully offer a good explanation to your interviewers as to why you were not given an offer.

Be flexible

Some firms, especially small firms, may be reluctant to hire you without getting to know you first. If you feel that an offer is not forthcoming for that reason, consider letting them know you are flexible. Here are some ways you can show your flexibility and let the firm get to know you better. First, you can ask the firm to hire you during the school year to do part-time work for an hourly fee. Second, if you have some time between graduation and studying for the bar, or if you are taking a year off to clerk, ask the firm to hire you for a few weeks as a summer intern after your 3L year. This way, if they really like you, you may have a job lined up at the end of that summer. Offering flexibility is a good way to show your interviewers how determined and interested you are in working for them.

Whether you are interviewing as a 1L, 2L, or 3L, be prepared to explain why you are interested in a particular employer and show that you have ties to a prospective area. Be flexible with regard to job opportunities, location, and practice areas. Finally, remember to sell yourself to your interviewers, share the positive aspects about your former employers, and prepare for your interviews thoroughly.

QuickReview

✓ Emphasize your ties to the geographic area where your employer is located and your desire to stay there long-term.

✓ Try not to restrict yourself to a particular practice area, type of employer, or location.

✓ Never criticize a former employer or a law professor who gave you a poor grade.

✓ Do not misrepresent that you have an offer, but do not offer negative information unless you are asked.

✓ Emphasize your skills, experience, and extracurricular activities during the interview to make up for a perceived lack of experience.

✓ Be prepared to explain your reasons for interviewing with a particular employer.

✓ Use mock interviews to prepare.

Chapter 22

CLERKSHIP INTERVIEWS

❧✗✗✗❧

Clerkship opportunities are rare, and interviews for them are difficult to get. Most judges receive hundreds of applications per opening. Your chances for success depend first on your application materials, and second on your interviewing skills. Accordingly, this chapter goes beyond addressing how to excel in clerkship interviews and discusses how to help you get them in the first place.

Make Your Application Stand Out

When hundreds of applications flood the chambers in the fall, opening and reading them can be quite overwhelming for judges and clerks, which is why some applications never receive the attention they deserve. Here is what you can do to make your application stand out.

First, if you mail your application, organize your materials logically. After a cover letter, the first thing the judge (or his or her clerks) will look for is a resume. Next, they will reach for a transcript. Place your writing sample and references at the back of the packet. If you are applying through the online application system (OSCAR), these materials will be sorted automatically.

Second, keep your cover letter concise. Beware of long, one-sentence paragraphs with grammatical errors and unnecessary information. But "concise" does not mean "dry." If there is something in your background that may help the judge relate to your application, briefly recite that fact in your cover letter.

Do not sound self-centered, deprecatory, or beggarly, and do not write an autobiography. Instead, explain briefly why you want to clerk for this particular judge. Avoid introductory paragraphs such as these:

"I am not the editor-in-chief of the Harvard Law Review or even number one in my class; nonetheless, I ask that you accept this letter as a confirmation of my promise to you that, if given the opportunity, I will be the hardest working law clerk that has ever served in your chambers."

"Approximately two years before the date of this letter my wife, my son and I moved from Jackson, Mississippi, to Atlanta, Georgia, so that I could attend law school there. I am writing to you in hopes of obtaining a clerkship position as I believe the position will further my pursuit of learning the practice of law and having a successful legal career."

Third, proofread your materials very carefully. Typos and punctuation errors are rarely, if ever, forgiven.

Fourth, always include a transcript, and list your class standing and GPA in your resume (unless it is really low). Clerks and judges are often too busy to sort through pages and pages of applications in an effort to locate this information. Very often, a resume that omits a GPA automatically goes into the rejection pile.

Fifth, do whatever you can to ensure that your letters of recommendation are included in your packet rather than mailed separately. Keep in mind that recommendations can break the tie between two equally strong candidates. Ask your recommenders to avoid boilerplate language and to personalize the letters by mentioning your strengths, personality traits, and strong writing skills.

Sixth, make sure your writing sample is short. Excerpts are fine, as long as you provide the context to set them up; oversized law review articles, articles in a published form, and samples that have clearly been edited, are unacceptable.

> Byron, a former clerk, once came across a writing sample that sent him into a stupor. The student used an appellate brief purportedly filed with the U.S. Supreme Court as her writing sample! Clearly this wasn't the student's original work, and her application went straight to the rejection pile.

Finally, unless instructed to do so, do not fax your application, do not mail it multiple times, do not e-mail it to the chambers, and do not call the chambers indiscriminately. They will likely turn down your application simply out of annoyance or fear that you are unbalanced. Persistent inquiry, which shows determination, is one thing; harassment and obnoxiousness is another.

Calling the Chambers

You were probably told that it is almost never okay to call the chambers. It is true, with one exception: If you live in a different city and plan to be in the same geographical area as the judge, do not hesitate to call the chambers and ask whether he or she would be willing to interview you while you are there. One of the reasons judges interview so few applicants is the cost of travel. So if you are going to be in the area anyway, call the judges in that area. You are likely to be turned down most of the time, but it only takes one interview to get an offer! Just remember, your phone call will be received better if you are polite, apologetic, and brief.

Timing

Many federal judges follow *The Law Clerk Hiring Plan*, which asserts that student applicants must mail their applications, and interviews must take place after a certain date in the fall. It is important to remember that the plan applies only to law students. So if you have graduated, or if you are applying for state court clerkships or federal clerkships with judges who do not follow the plan, apply early to improve your odds.

If you get an interview, always schedule it as soon as possible. Although some judges do not make offers until they interview all the candidates, most judges make them on a rolling basis. Some even give on-the-spot "exploding offers" (in which you enthusiastically accept the offer right away or it is rescinded). As a result, they may no longer have openings when your interview rolls around. Therefore, take the first available interview slot and hop on a plane. Although you will probably have little say about the time of the day, try to aim for the morning. There is less risk of a delay, a need to reschedule, or interruptions. We should add that some judges interview candidates at odd hours (such as 6 a.m. or midnight), but typically you cannot be choosy.

Preparing for a Clerkship Interview

Do not treat all judges the same! Some judges estimate that less than half of interviewees actually prepare for their interviews or know anything about the interviewers. If you want to make an impression, prepare. During your interview, remember to discuss the judge's opinions to show the judge that you are well aware of his or her decisions, writing style, and ideology. Judges love to talk about themselves and about the cases they have authored. But they are also wary of candidates who flatter them too much. So personalize your research, but only bring up relevant information when appropriate, and do not overdo flattery.

Check if the judge has published any articles and, if so, read them carefully. They can serve as a great conversation topic. Just be mindful that once you bring up a certain legal topic, you may be expected to demonstrate your expertise in it. It is also a good idea to skim any news articles about the judge or his or her decisions, but stay away from discussing any negative publicity you may have discovered.

Asking former clerks for insights into the judge's way of thinking, hiring preferences, and possible interview questions is a great way to prepare; some judges are genuinely flattered by that. But remember that the clerks will almost always relate your conversation to the judge, so phrase your questions carefully. Although most judges do not mind you contacting former clerks, they advise against contacting current clerks to prevent any appearance of impropriety during the hiring process.

After you learn everything you can about the judge, jot down a list of possible questions. Be sure to write out your answers and practice answering questions in front of a mirror. These questions include, for example, questions about your reasons for going to law school, wanting to clerk, and wanting to move to a certain location.

Finally, sit down with your law school career counselors who may be able to share insights about your judge and help you prepare through mock interviews. Mock interviews can help you gain confidence and prepare you for challenging questions. Just remember to provide your "mock judge" with all relevant information so he or she can ask you meaningful questions. Be sure to also read Chapter 3 for details on how to prepare for clerkship interviews.

Possible Topics and Questions

Judges can ask you anything they want—they are judges. So prepare as much as you can, but be ready to think on your feet. Brush up on current events and read about recent Supreme Court decisions. Although most questions are relatively straightforward, sometimes judges prefer asking complex legal questions. For example, one judge asked a clerkship applicant about his thoughts on judicial activism. "Ju...what?" the poor kid almost asked. Another judge questioned an interviewee about recent Supreme Court oral arguments and her predictions regarding the outcomes.

Be prepared to answer more traditional interview questions, as well. For example: "Why do you want to clerk for me?" "What are your reasons for applying for a clerkship here?" "Where do you see yourself in five years?" and "What are your strngths and weaknesses?" When asking such questions, judges look for thoughtful answers that indicate that you are prepared, you know what the job entails, and you have realistic expectations about the job. Bluntness is not the best policy here! Do not answer the "why" question by saying (1) you want a resume booster; (2) you are applying because you do not know what you want to do yet; (3) the clerkship is your stepping stone to another position; or (4) you want an easy job because you are tired of billing hours. Whatever the question is, it gives you a clue as to what is really important to the judge, so listen carefully. Here are some good answers that can help you pass the test:

✓ "I want to clerk for you because you are a great mentor to your clerks."

✓ "I want to clerk for you because I will have a chance to work on a certain type of cases."

✓ "I have an interest in criminal work, and you allow your clerks to work on criminal cases."

✓ "I want to work at a smaller court where I can interact more with other clerks."

✓ "I want to be an appellate lawyer, and working with you will help me hone those skills."

Steer clear from initiating discussions about politics and religion, but realize that they are fair game for a judge. Some judges like to hire clerks with certain political opinions, or those who can simply voice an opinion. So if you are asked a question like this, do not dance around it; give a thoughtful and honest answer, and be prepared to defend your position. The judge will appreciate it more than an answer you think he or she wants to hear. At the same time, clerking requires an ability to keep an open mind, so be careful not to take an extreme position.

Finally, be prepared to address any weak spots on your resume. Whether it is the fact that you have never been published, your minor role on the journal, or a gap in your academic career, the judge is not going to miss it. In fact, his or her clerks will probably highlight it so that he or she remembers to ask you about it. Anticipate this question and figure out how to put a positive spin on your answer.

How a Judge May Test You

When asked about an ideal candidate at the interview stage, virtually all judges emphasize personality as the most important trait. They look for candidates who are well-rounded, who have life experience, who can display humanity and humility, who have a good sense of humor (without being inappropriate), and who can take a position without being disagreeable. All in all, they want someone who is a great fit. One judge describes his interviews this way: "I usually need to get through them quickly so I can get back to work. If a candidate makes me forget about the time and makes me think, 'What a nice way to spend a day!' he or she is the one who gets an offer."

Judges occasionally employ sophisticated interview strategies to test their applicants' personalities. Some judges, for example, start forming an opinion about a candidate during their initial phone conversation. They expect a professional answering machine recording, a polite tone, and eagerness in a candidate's voice. If any one of these components is missing, this may be enough for a judge to withdraw an interview offer. One judge we know is known for asking candidates trivia questions on such diverse subjects as history, geography, and literature. He wants his clerks to be well-rounded and knowledgeable, and he finds these questions helpful in identifying star applicants from lower-ranked schools.

Other judges watch a candidate carefully during the first few minutes of an interview, analyzing his or her dress code, body language, and demeanor. Says one federal judge, "When the candidate first walks into my chambers, I give him a choice where to sit. He can pick between such formal interview settings as my desk or a conference room table, or he can proceed to a casual corner with a sofa and two armchairs. I am looking for people who can relax, be upfront and casual, and who can have informal conversations with me. So the sofa is my top preference. To this day, I cannot think of a candidate who received an offer [who] didn't choose the sofa."

Not all judges look for clerks who are casual, though. Some judges are very formal and expect their candidates to be, as well. This is why it is so important to do your homework and to let your first impressions guide you. One judge we know of never talks during the first few minutes of the interview. When the candidate walks in, he or she is expected to do the talking. This puts incredible pressure on the candidate to initiate and carry on a conversation. The judge only hires those clerks who can withstand this "silent treatment."

Some judges also ask tricky questions. One court of appeals judge, for example, asks his clerkship applicants when they last spoke to their mother. You may not have guessed it, but the best answer (in this judge's opinion) is "10 minutes before this interview." This judge believes that a candidate who is close to his or her mother will be very loyal. Another judge always asks whether a candidate has anything to add at the end of the interview. To her, the most impressive answer is a sincere "I really want this job" or "There is one more thing...." Bad answers include "No, I do not have anything to add" or "Please, please hire me! I will do anything to get this job."

Asking Your Own Questions

You can ace the interview by showing that you are a well-rounded candidate with a great personality. Watch your demeanor and exhibit confidence and humility. To show your sincere interest, always ask questions. Good questions to ask the judge include:

✓ "How do you like being a judge?"

✓ "How did you decide to become a judge?"

✓ "What was the most important thing that helped you become a judge?"

✓ "What do you expect from your clerks?"

✓ "What are you looking for in clerkship applicants?"

✓ "What is your mentorship style?"

✓ "Do you prefer to closely guide your clerks through the writing process, or do you discuss their projects after they are completed?"

✓ "Do your clerks work on both civil and criminal matters?"

✓ "Do you keep in touch with your former clerks? Do you encourage them to keep in touch?"

Here is a list of possible questions for the judge's former clerks:

✓ "What does the judge look for in his/her clerks?"

✓ "What were your responsibilities as a clerk?"

✓ "Does the judge encourage clerks to voice opinions in cases in which you disagree with the outcome?"

✓ "What did you find most challenging about your job?"

✓ "What was your favorite part about clerking?"

✓ "Did you have an opportunity to work on both civil and criminal matters?"

✓ "What were the most important things this clerkship taught you?"

Responding to an Offer

Surprisingly, less than one-third of interviewees send thank-you letters to judges. Yet, according to judges, these letters can make all the difference when there is a tie. Immediately after the interview, mail a brief formal thank-you letter to the judge. It should be typed, though a handwritten note at the bottom is a nice touch. If you also met the judge's staff, send them thank-you letters as well. A good, error-free thank-you letter will often convince the judge to choose you over other candidates. Most judges say that even a brief thank-you letter is better than no letter at all. But, ideally, it should be personalized by mentioning something that was discussed at the interview.

Despite whatever you may have heard to the contrary, you *can* decline a clerkship offer. But only do it if you have compelling reasons or if a judge encouraged you to think about the offer. In all other circumstances, if you receive an offer from a judge, it is a good idea to accept immediately, even if you are expecting offers from other judges. Keep in mind that a judge may be busy or simply impatient, so if you must ask for an extension, be extremely diplomatic and do so promptly. Return his or her calls right away, and if you are traveling during the interviewing season, remember to state as much on your voicemail message. Some judges are afraid of losing the best candidates and may grow impatient if you take too long to respond.

> While Ryan was on his way to a second clerkship inter-
> view, he received a voicemail from a judge who interviewed
> him a few days before, extending an offer. Because Ryan
> was still in midair, however, he could neither check nor respond
> to the judge's message. Growing impatient, the judge called back
> an hour later and rescinded the offer. So, by the time Ryan
> landed, he had two messages—one giving him an offer and one
> notifying him it had expired.

Getting a clerkship is important, but there is only so much you can do
to get one. Although it is advisable to be thoroughly prepared for your
clerkship interviews, do not agonize excessively over the interviewing process. Your priority is to be likeable, genuine, and professional. To some
judges, "professional" means "comfortable enough to sit on a couch during an interview"; to others, it means "extremely formal." The only way to
figure this out is by doing your homework and by trusting your intuition.

QuickReview

✓ Make your clerkship application easy to read, and remember to
   include your GPA on your resume.

✓ Send letters of reference together with your application packet.

✓ Ask your recommenders to say one or two personal things about
   you.

✓ Only call the judge's chambers if you will be traveling to the area
   and want to ask for an interview.

✓ Prepare for your clerkship interviews thoroughly, using all possible resources.

✓ Do not share your views on politics and controversial subjects
   unless you are invited to do so.

✓ Know everything there is to know about the judge and his or her
   opinions, and do your best to demonstrate how prepared you
   are.

✓ Send personalized thank-you letters immediately after the interview.

Chapter 23

GOVERNMENT INTERVIEWS

The competition for government jobs is stiff. Although the work done in different government agencies varies greatly, there are two common denominators when it comes to getting a government position. First, it requires thorough research and preparation; second, with a few exceptions, most government positions require prior work experience or relevant skills. Keep this in mind as you contemplate your career options in the government and prepare for your interviews.

Preparation and Experience Are Key

Your number-one research assignment is to determine when to begin preparing to apply for a government position. An entry-level position in a small government office in a rural location may not require that much preparation; meanwhile, becoming an assistant U.S. attorney in Los Angeles or New York may, depending on your level of experience, require years of preparation. Such preparation may include clerking, obtaining trial experience, and doing public service work, in addition to conducting thorough research of what the position entails. Likewise, if your goal is to become a staff attorney with the Securities and Exchange Commission, it would behoove you to have at least a few years of experience practicing in the areas of securities and corporate law.

According to one high-ranking government attorney, preparation is key for government interviews. By the time the candidate is sitting in her office for an interview, the candidate should "know precisely what we do here, know the agency's purpose and mission, and know what the staff attorneys do." A number of high-level federal prosecutors echoed the same sentiment. To convince them to hire you, you must demonstrate that you know what your future job will entail. It is not enough to come into an interview with a general understanding of the job requirements. You must indicate that you know and understand what you will be doing on a daily basis, either from

your conversations with people who currently work there, from independent research, or, ideally, both. If you do not know anyone who holds a
similar government position, letting your interviewers know that you would
like to meet people who can tell you more about the job will help convey
your strong interest. In short, the more you know about the job, the more
confident your interviewers will be that you can master it.

> Chuck, a lawyer from Alaska, interviewed for a position
> with a U.S. attorney's office in Texas. When the interviewer
> asked him why he wanted the job, he mumbled some-
> thing about liking warm weather. Then, when the interviewers
> tried to explain to him that 90 percent of the cases they pros-
> ecuted were border-related crimes, he exclaimed, "I had no
> idea you are so close to the border!" The interviewers were not
> impressed with his failure to do his homework. Despite stellar
> credentials, Chuck did not get an offer.

Begin your research by looking at the agency's Website and literature
for a description of what they do. In addition, look at the agency's press
releases. For instance, if you are applying to a U.S. attorney's office, look
at press releases about recent victories, trials, convictions, and indictments.
One or more of your interviewers could have worked on those cases, and
would likely be very impressed if you brought them up.

Finally, do not be afraid to network and request informational interviews. Government lawyers are people, too. You can meet them at local
bar association dinners or civic events. You can ask them about their jobs,
take them out to lunch, explain that you are considering a career in their
office, and ask them for more information. Consider asking them "What
do you think I need to know about this position?" "What have you found
most rewarding about it?" or "What's the toughest thing about your job?"

Ask people who hold positions similar to the one you seek for informational interviews (we recommend calling in this case, because e-mails are
more likely to be ignored). For example, leave the following message: "Hello
Ms./Mr.____. My name is____, and I'm calling because I'm interviewing in
another city for the position you currently hold. I'd greatly appreciate 10
minutes of your time for a few questions so I can soak up your knowledge
about the job. If you'd be so kind as to lend your time for that, it would help
me gain a deeper knowledge of what this position entails. You can reach me
at the following number."

By gathering as much information as possible, you will impress your
interviewers with your commitment, thoroughness, and motivation. During your interviews, do not forget to mention that you conducted research
and contacted people in similar positions to learn more about the job. This
will demonstrate your future commitment to the job.

Answering the "Why" Question

Many government attorneys have distinct career paths that brought them to their current positions. Some started their careers with federal clerkships, some in private practice, some with different government agencies. However, they all had specific reasons for wanting to get a government job. When you are asked why you want the job, you had better have a researched, thoughtful, and sincere answer prepared. To do this effectively, determine why you want to become a government lawyer. When communicating your reasons to the interviewers, avoid those that may raise red flags; for example:

✓ "I want to join your office because it is prestigious."

✓ "I want to build my resume."

✓ "I would like to get some trial experience here and then return to private practice."

✓ "I would like a 9-to-5 job, without the billable-hour requirements."

✓ "I think I would be a good fit for this job because I like being independent, and I hear your attorneys have a lot of autonomy."

You get the idea. Emphasize that you are serious about the purpose behind the work, that you are willing to work hard, and that you intend to stay long-term. If your interviewers get a sense that you plan to use this job as a stepping stone, you will not get an offer.

Although all employers want candidates who will be committed to their work, the government needs this quality even more so. The government's budget is limited, and the pay is lower than it is in private practice. In light of this, applicants must demonstrate their motivation to do their work well in addition to their desire to advance within the agency. Says one federal prosecutor: "One of the best answers you can give us is to say that you hope to have an opportunity to stay with us once your two-year term expires." Additionally, you want to answer the "why" question by explaining what steps you took to ensure your success as a government lawyer (public service, community work, pro bono, relevant work experience, and so on).

Exhibit Realistic Expectations

Every government agency gets their share of applicants who think they will set the world on fire. A district attorney's office may get an entry-level applicant who talks about how great it will be to try a felony murder. The U.S. Attorney's Office may get someone talking about bringing down corrupt politicians. The State Department could have someone talking about major changes in foreign policy. In reality, you will not be doing any of this during your first couple of years as a government lawyer. In fact, your likeliest lot is prosecuting misdemeanors, trying small drug-related crimes, or writing memos and appellate briefs.

Know exactly what you will be doing if you get the job, and communicate this understanding to your interviewers in order to show that you will not quit after two weeks because you find the work too difficult or mundane. You will greatly increase your chances by conveying to your interviewers that you know what to expect, and that you are excited about this opportunity.

Interview Logistics

Different government agencies and offices have different ways of conducting interviews. Some interview in several stages: First you meet more junior attorneys and then, should you progress to the next stage, you meet more senior people. Other offices may conduct day-long interviews, in which you have three or four meetings in the morning, a break for lunch, and then four or five meetings in the afternoon. For many government jobs, candidates are questioned by two interviewers at the same time. Additionally, it is not unusual for applicants to interview for government positions months and even years in advance of their desired start date. It can often be a long process, so relax and be patient.

Otherwise, government interviews are conducted much in the same way as they are in private practice. A government office typically employs a recruiting manager who will be your primary contact, explain the process to you, introduce you to your interviewers, and answer questions. Treat this person with great respect. Remember, he or she sees applicants like you (or better) every day, and his or her opinion is usually highly valued by the agency.

Anticipate Questions

Although most firms encourage their interviewers to be politically correct and follow a standard interviewing protocol, government agencies, which have an abundant applicant pool, are less concerned about scaring off candidates by asking challenging questions. This means that their questions can be much less predictable and much more challenging.

Hypothetical questions and requests for impromptu performances are not uncommon, so do not be surprised if you get thrown a curve ball. For example, your interviewers may ask you to deliver a brief opening statement, quickly write a short piece on a certain subject, or discuss whether you would disclose incriminating evidence to your opponent after the close of discovery. Government lawyers often ask challenging questions in efforts to test your confidence, skills, and preparedness. In large part, these questions are designed to analyze your performance under pressure and (less often) evaluate your actual skills. So focus on giving well-structured, coherent, and confident answers without sounding nervous or unprepared. Here are just a few examples:

✓ "How would you handle the pressure of having to argue three cases in one day?"

✓ "In two minutes or less, discuss all the legal issues you see in [insert top news story of the month here]."

✓ "How would you feel about prosecuting a single mother of three?"

✓ "Opposing counsel takes a personal shot at you by saying something defamatory in open court. How do you respond?"

✓ "What is the single most important reason why we should hire you?"

As you can probably tell, most of these questions do not presuppose any particular response. They are asked to put you on the spot and to see how you fare. Nevertheless, there are wrong answers to some of these questions. For example, saying that you would be reluctant to prosecute a sympathetic defendant or would respond in kind to an opposing counsel's attack may raise the interviewer's eyebrows. Try to approach these questions from your interviewer's point of view, and do your best to show you can withstand the pressure.

Be Confident, Not Arrogant

You have researched your desired position, polished your resume, put together an interview game plan, and are ready to go. You have a dark suit on (but not a very expensive one—remember, your interviewers live on a government salary!), and you are ready to shine. Just do not think you can outshine your interviewers. Government interviewers stress the importance of exhibiting confidence and humility without sounding arrogant. According to one high-level government attorney who interviews candidates daily, "Arrogance indicates the candidate's inability to work in a team, which is essential for government attorneys. We are only as strong as our weakest lawyer. So we look for candidates who can assist their colleagues when necessary."

Getting an offer for a government position requires you to convince your interviewers that you are team-oriented, that you value working even on small cases, and that you do not treat the first few years of the government experience as "paying dues" for getting to work on more prestigious, high-profile matters. No matter how impressive your credentials are, tuck away your sense of entitlement and express enthusiasm and sincere gratitude for being considered for the job. Finally, do not forget to emphasize that your interest is not primarily in having shorter hours; show that you are prepared to work hard and under pressure, and that you see yourself working in this position for many years to come.

QuickReview

✓ Research information about specific government jobs well in advance of applying.

✓ Know enough about the agency to be able to discuss it at the interview.

✓ Make it a point to meet at least a few people who have either held a similar position in the past or are currently working in that office.

✓ Develop a realistic expectation of your future job responsibilities.

✓ Make sure to convey to your interviewer that you know what the job entails; ask for further information when necessary.

✓ Be patient with the application process no matter how lengthy it is.

✓ Prepare a researched and thoughtful answer to the "why" question.

✓ Be confident without sounding arrogant, tackle challenging questions, and emphasize teamwork.

Chapter 24

LATERAL INTERVIEWS

❦

In a healthy economy, the demand for experienced young lawyers is usually high. It is not uncommon for associates to receive daily calls from headhunters trying to recruit them. Lateral candidates have options: They can move up to higher-ranked firms, go to smaller firms with better partnership prospects, or obtain in-house or part-time positions. Many take advantage of these opportunities. Some studies estimate that more than 80 percent of attorneys change jobs at least once within five years of graduation. In fact, it is now completely acceptable for junior attorneys to move several times before finally settling down. With the growing mobility in the legal profession, lateral interviews are becoming significantly more important.

Are You Ready?

Lateral interviewing is a very demanding process; it takes a great deal of time, energy, and effort. In light of this, do not interview if you are not ready, and do not interview "just in case." Evaluate your likelihood of moving, and only apply for a job if you are ready to make a move within six months or less. Once you decide to leave, leave. Do not succumb to pressure or flattery from your current employer; working there after you had "strayed" may end up being like a marriage from hell.

Lisa, who worked in a small legal market, interviewed "just to look around." After she announced she was leaving, her supervisors convinced her to stay. Nevertheless, she was subjected to a terrible work environment, and months later her employer gave her the boot. The firms that previously gave her offers said they could no longer hire her because she did not take her job search—or their time—seriously.

It is one thing to turn down an offer because you have joined another firm. It is another thing to waste the firm's time and resources and tell them you are not ready to move after all.

> Jackson interviewed with every firm in town and received offers to join them as a lateral. But he changed his mind and decided to stay. When he tried to interview with these firms again a year later, he did not receive a single interview. No one took him seriously anymore.

Moreover, by interviewing before you are ready, you may inadvertently alert your employer to your disloyalty.

> Joanna, a mid-level associate in Los Angeles, applied to another firm because she wanted to see if the grass was indeed greener. While interviewing, she discovered she liked her current firm more and decided to stay after all. But her strategy backfired when she ran into a colleague from her current firm during one of her interviews. In her freshly pressed suit, with a resume in hand, and having called in sick at work, Joanna had no choice but to admit she was interviewing. Unfortunately, this meant she now had to leave, whether she wanted to or not.

Logistics

Lateral interviewing is a bit different from on-campus and callback interviewing. First and foremost, as you probably realize, there is much more at stake when you interview as a lateral. This is especially true if you practice in a small legal market and have limited lateral opportunities available to you. Because of this, you must take the interviewing process even more seriously than you did in law school.

Once you apply for a lateral position and receive an interview, be prepared to have several rounds of interviews. At many firms, you will first undergo a screening interview with one or two attorneys at the firm, usually partners. Think of them as bouncers—they are there to make sure you are not a psycho before they let you in for a full round of fun.

The next step in the lateral interviewing process is similar to a callback interview. You will spend four to six hours meeting anywhere from six to eight attorneys. One thing to remember during this stage is that you should focus most of your energy on the partners. They will be the key decision-makers in this process. If even one of them does not like you, you probably will not get an offer. Meanwhile, your interviews with associates may carry slightly less weight. Nevertheless, be pleasant, deferential, and collegial with everyone. When interviewing with an associate and a partner at the same time, do not disregard the associate in your efforts to focus on the partner, because you may come off as rude.

At most firms, the lateral interviewing process will end after two rounds of interviews. But some employers require as many as three rounds. At small firms, you may have more than three rounds and end up meeting every attorney at the firm. Lateral interviews are long and exhausting, so keep this in mind if you are thinking about interviewing at a large number of firms within a short period of time. Consider starting with your top three firms and scheduling interviews with the remaining firms two to three weeks away. This way, if you have offers from your top-choice firms, you may not have to interview with your "second-tier" potential employers. On the other hand, if you have very limited interviewing experience, you should always interview with your bottom-choice employers first to help you gain experience before going for your dream job.

Strict Scrutiny

Lateral interviews are generally more comprehensive and thorough than interviews for summer associate positions. The reason for this is the employer's need to scrutinize lateral applicants. Employers are much more cautious when interviewing laterals because they cannot hire them on a trial basis. Rather, they must make long-term hiring decisions with limited time and information.

Furthermore, most candidates who interview for lateral positions do so while still working for their current employers. They do not want to advertise the fact that they are interviewing. This presents an additional challenge for potential employers, who must honor the candidate's request to keep his or her application confidential. Consequently, potential employers cannot ask everyone in town for feedback about the candidate; instead, they must be careful not to impact the candidate's current job status.

A law firm will typically run a thorough background check before they hire you as a lateral. They will probably know your credit score and debt status better than you do. From criminal background checks and credit reports to reference checks, law firms take lateral interviews very seriously. Sometimes too seriously, it seems.

In Howard's example, the firm where he interviewed for a lateral position asked him to fill out a 20-page questionnaire. He then signed a waiver for a background check, which generated a 30-page report from every state, city, and county where he had ever lived. The background check results also reproduced Howard's credit history, including his current debt. To check references, the firm sent an e-mail to every single attorney in its 120-person office, asking if they had any information about the candidate. Granted, the e-mail indicated that this information was strictly confidential; but of course the old firm found out. Fortunately for Howard, he received an offer from the new firm right before an unpleasant conversation with his old employer. But the process was nerve-wracking.

Your lateral interviewing experience may be a bit different if you are working with a headhunter. See Chapter 26 for an in-depth discussion of this subject. Firms usually trust the headhunters to do all the groundwork, and you may not even be asked for references if you are applying through a recruiter. But, in any event, be prepared.

Checking References

Many firms will want to call references at your current firm. If you are concerned about having a job while interviewing, you should ask your interviewers to call your references *after* you receive and accept an offer. Just be aware that many government employers, as well as some firms and in-house employers, will insist on calling references before making you an offer. Ask if they would be willing to rely on former colleagues who left your current firm. Think about this in advance and have a list of references ready for this occasion. It may also be worth mentioning all the good feedback you have received from your current employer, which indicates you are well-liked and may help you get out of having to provide references.

Your references will usually have no impact on whether you receive an offer, and they will almost never be used to rescind an offer unless something has gone terribly wrong at your current job. But be aware that legal employers check references very carefully when you apply for a lateral position. Never make misrepresentations, and make sure your story is consistent with what you expect your references to say.

Know Your Reasons for Interviewing

You will be asked why you are interviewing over and over again during lateral interviews because all employers will want to know why you desire to leave your current job. In fact, this is the single most important question during lateral interviews, and your answer will directly impact whether you get an offer. Practice your answer in advance, with friends or in front of the mirror, and make sure it sounds convincing.

Your real reasons for interviewing probably have something to do with being treated poorly, getting stuck doing paralegal work, or not seeing daylight since Labor Day weekend. From the employer's perspective, however, these are not good reasons. Therefore, when you discuss why you are leaving your current firm, the appropriate good reasons are relocation, the desire to move to a firm of a different size, the desire to work at a certain department, the desire for an opportunity to work with more attorneys, or your goal of working at a firm where you can develop a certain specialty. Come up with two positive reasons for interviewing and mention them both.

> Alyssa recently made a lateral move from a firm where she was stuck doing document review to another firm, which offered her significant writing and deposition experience. During her interview, she steered clear of discussing her bitter feelings about doc review. Instead, she focused on the fact that the new firm offered her an opportunity to develop a specialty in insurance defense, which she could not do at her current firm. She also noted that she wanted an opportunity to work with more attorneys prior to developing a specialty, which, again, she could not do at the current firm. She aced the interview and got an offer.

Discussions About Specialty

Lately, more and more firms are discussing a specialty with lateral associates. This includes even the most junior associates with less than two years of experience. For many firms, it is no longer sufficient to be a good litigator or a good corporate attorney and ride your way to a partnership. Now, attorneys must develop a specialty earlier in their careers. Keep in mind that the mere fact that you got a lateral interview means that you are probably being considered for a position in a specific department or group. Before they make you an offer, chances are your interviewers will want to zero in on the type of work you want to do in order to find out whether you will be a good match for the type of work they offer. Finally, remember that the firm may not be hiring for a certain department due to a slowdown. If you say you have several specialties in mind, the firm will undoubtedly appreciate your flexibility.

Questions About Experience

Employers will always want to know about your experience. From your perspective, this is yet another reason not to complain about too much due diligence or document review. Who wants to hire an associate who knows only how to browse through legal documents? Instead, emphasize the substantive experience you have gained at your current firm.

In fact, you should sit down before your interview, review your time sheets, and write down all of the things you did in the last year or two that involved substantive work. Even if you spent three-quarters of your time on meaningless assignments, you will discover that you still probably managed to do enough substantive work to be able to bring it up in your interview. (Just be careful not to reveal any confidential client information.)

Questions About Career Goals

This topic rarely comes up during interviews, but as a good interviewee you should proactively address it. Here is why: A desire to make a lateral move can sometimes be perceived as stemming from lack of a definite career plan or prospects. From the employer's perspective, you have tried working at one firm, did not like it, and now want to "sample" another one. If time permits, therefore, you should try to dispel this myth by tackling it head on. You can do this while answering a question, complimenting the interviewer or the firm, or asking about your career prospects.

To address your interviewers' concerns, tell them where you see yourself in the next five to 10 years. Letting them know that you see yourself working at this firm for years to come will also communicate that you have a long-term career goal, and that you are serious about your desire to grow professionally within the organization. Likewise, discussing your desire to make partner and develop a specialty will score you major points. In most cases, your interviewer wants to see a commitment on your part, demonstrated by (1) your desire to work as an attorney for many years, (2) your desire to make a partner, (3) your desire to develop a specialty, and (4) your wish to remain in the same geographical location. Focusing on the future shows that you are serious about making a long-term commitment. Your interviewers will not necessarily assume that you are a "sure thing" because of this, but they will see the benefit in hiring someone who wants to try.

Questions About Other Firms

You may be asked where else you are interviewing. You do not have to give a complete answer. Full disclosure never works to your advantage in answering the dreaded "how many" question. We suggest acknowledging that you are, in fact, interviewing with other firms, without specifying which ones or how many. Never lie about your job prospects, especially if you name names. Your interviewer may know someone at a firm you name and decide to verify the information. A lie about an offer or an interview with another employer can ruin your chances and damage your reputation.

If pressed, name at least two and no more than four firms. If you say you are only interviewing with one firm, your new employers may feel no need to hurry and give you an offer, or they may get the feeling that you are not that great of a candidate. Likewise, if you tell them you applied to a whole bunch of firms, they may think you are not serious or confident enough. This range of numbers shows that you are seriously looking but not applying like crazy for jobs all around the country.

If you do not have any other interviews lined up yet, tell your interviewer about the firms you are interested in. If your interviewer follows up and asks you whether you are interviewing with them, you could say, "Not yet. Because I am very interested in your firm, I wanted to wait until after our interview to schedule interviews with other firms." Because there is always a chance you may interview with them later, you are not misrepresenting anything.

Finally, if you are interviewing for firm and government positions at the same time, or if you are interviewing with different departments at different firms, do not disclose this information to your interviewers. Your "diverse" interviewing portfolio may jeopardize your offer because it suggests a desire to explore alternative careers, and can show a lack of commitment.

Never Badmouth an Employer

Last but not least, we will leave you with the most important advice of all: Never, under any circumstances, say anything bad about an employer. We have heard numerous stories about lateral associates who looked great on paper, passed the screening interviews with flying colors, but who broke down when they were asked about a current or previous employer. In one case, a junior associate went into a 20-minute rant about how terrible her old firm was, how unpleasant the people were, and how she could not wait to get out of there. In another example, a mid-level associate badmouthed three partners at his former firm—people who happened to be good friends with his interviewer. These interviews resulted in some awkward moments, and there was no chance whatsoever that these candidates would receive offers after having given such negative feedback.

Remember, too, that even in large markets, this is a small world. Whatever you say today may be used against you in the legal community tomorrow. In short, the most successful lateral candidates are the ones who find positive things to say about their current and former employers.

One partner at a small firm told us that he was most impressed with an associate who started answering a question by mentioning how much she enjoyed working at her current firm, how many friends she had made there, and how much she had learned there as an attorney. Only then did she note that, unfortunately, she had to leave because her department was downsizing, and she was afraid she would no longer be able to receive the same mentorship as before. In truth, the associate held a grudge against her firm for giving better work to another associate while she was stuck doing all the dirty work. But she found positive things to say about the firm, and her strategy paid off. The partner in this story personally called her to extend an offer the very same day!

Lateral interviewing is a complicated and perilous dance. Fortunately, most firms have developed a fairly predictable *modus operandi* when it comes to lateral candidates. In terms of the mechanics—timing issues, the confidentiality of your job application, background checks, discussing your job prospects, and accepting an offer—simply follow the steps presented in this chapter. Decide ahead of time how you will answer questions about specialty, experience, and career goals. When discussing current and former employers, focus on the positive.

QuickReview

✓ Do not interview for a lateral position unless you are ready to make the move.

✓ Take lateral interviewing very seriously; there is more at stake here than there was when you were in law school.

✓ If you indicate in your cover letter that your job application is confidential, your interviewers will likely treat it as such.

✓ Have a good story ready about why you want to make a move.

✓ Use your legal experience as both a way to sell yourself and a way to explain your desire to make a lateral move.

✓ Tell your interviewer about your desire to develop a certain specialty, but remember to mention that you are flexible.

✓ Never say anything even remotely negative about a current or former employer.

Chapter 25

GOING IN-HOUSE

The process of making a move in-house is complex. There is often very little information available about in-house job openings, compensation structures, and employers' backgrounds. This is why working with a headhunter during this stage of your career has significant perks. Legal recruiters, especially those specifically catering to the in-house job market, are an invaluable resource when it comes to finding out about job openings and developing solid connections with in-house employers. Remember that your personality and experience are the keys to going in-house. Do not treat in-house interviews as you would firm interviews. Focus on making connections with your interviewers, showing a genuine interest in the company, and demonstrating how your experience can benefit them in the long run.

Unique Aspects of In-House Positions

Many attorneys dream about moving in-house one day, expecting 9-to-5 hours, a family-friendly environment, stability, and a high income. But the reality is that in-house jobs vary just as much as firm jobs do. You may be working with a large group of people, or you may be the only junior associate in a group working with three senior attorneys. You may be making significantly more in bonus and compensation, or you may be offered less than your starting salary at a firm. Your "family-friendly" in-house gig may require you to travel or work on weekends. After seeking an intellectually challenging position, you may be disappointed to discover that your in-house job involves very little substantive legal work. The bottom line is, do your research before interviewing and accepting an offer so that you are not blindsided.

> Kelly recently accepted an in-house position at a small start-up company. Although she is optimistic about her career prospects, she admits that her job is far from what

she had expected. As a senior associate at a prestigious New York firm, she was often working on the weekends. But she was also well-compensated for every hour billed, receiving a hefty bonus at the end of the year on top of her $200,000-plus salary. And, if she disliked working with a certain partner, she had no difficulty turning to someone else for work in the large corporate department of her firm. Things are different now. Kelly reports to two attorneys and, when things go wrong, she is the first to be blamed. Although her supervisors are friendly, they do not hesitate to send her assignments on the weekends. Kelly also recently discovered that her job involves traveling— something she was not aware of when she interviewed for the position shortly after the birth of her son. Kelly admits that sometimes she secretly wishes she could go back to her firm life.

Most in-house positions do carry such benefits as work stability, no billable-hour requirements, and a reduced schedule. But there are also plenty of in-house jobs with demanding work schedules and reduced compensation. Before moving in-house, always investigate what your new position will entail.

The Interview Process

Competition for in-house jobs is intense. A good in-house position at a known company can easily generate more than 100 resume submissions and result in 20 interviews. The top seven or eight candidates are then invited for the second round of interviews, three or four for the third round, and so forth. The further along you are in the interviewing process, the less people you will be competing against.

In-house interviewers place a great deal of emphasis on your personality and prior work experience. Thus your ultimate goal is to convince them that you have a great personality, and that they can benefit from your skills and experience. Depending on the company's size, you may have as few as one or as many as five callbacks. You are also likely to meet most of the people who will work with you directly. During a particularly intensive interviewing process, you can also expect to meet the higher-ups at the company.

Do not be surprised if you meet the same attorneys in each round of interviews. This often happens if there is a question about your candidacy, and the interviewers want to meet you again to determine how they can advocate effectively on your behalf (if they like you), or whether they should support your candidacy at all (if they are on the fence). Just act naturally and put your best foot forward each time.

It is also not uncommon to be interviewed by attorneys who have less seniority than you do. You can score major points with them by researching their bios and including a bit of flattery in your interviews. Additionally, because junior lawyers seek out people who will be good mentors, remember to discuss your mentorship style, the type and quality of work you would be willing to delegate, and the amount of feedback you would offer. Finally, treat everyone, including junior attorneys and support staff, with utmost respect. Exhibiting arrogance to interviewees or failing to acknowledge secretaries can easily cost you an offer.

The job titles and duties of in-house interviewers vary from company to company. Know what they are, and be aware of the reporting structure. If it turns out that your interviewer is high up in the reporting structure but you have more years of experience, you should proactively address this issue with that interviewer. Specifically, you must convince him or her that (1) you will not be a threat, (2) you are comfortable with the reporting structure, and (3) you are okay with working for someone less senior. Here is one way to address it: "I understand I would be reporting to you. At this stage of my career, it is important for me to get along with my team and do challenging work. I am not looking to move up rapidly or be a superstar. I am easy to get along with, and I have no problem with this reporting structure."

The Importance of Homework

Initial research is important. It helps you decide whether to leap into the in-house market, it allows you to narrow down the list of companies that may hire you, and it helps you convince the employer of your genuine interest. This is where working with a headhunter comes in handy, as he or she can point you to the right sources, tell you about the employer's background, and help you develop an interest. But working with a headhunter does not mean getting your research done for you.

> Keith, a cum laude graduate of a Top 10 school, sat casually in his chair while his headhunter tried to help him prep for his in-house interview. "Keith," asked the headhunter, "Why do you want to work for this company?" Unprepared and somewhat puzzled, Keith slumped in his chair and said, "You tell me."

If you do what Keith did, you will never find a job at a reputable company. Although being a top candidate may get you an offer from a top-tier firm, even given a certain level of arrogance or unpreparedness on your part, much more is required to secure a great in-house position. Good grades alone will not cut it—you must be prepared to explain why you are interested in working there and convince your interviewers that your interest is genuine.

Researching companies can be more difficult than researching firms because there is usually less information available online. So be prepared to spend significantly more time preparing for in-house interviews. Never use a lack of information as an excuse not to be prepared! The only successful way to an in-house position is through in-depth research, extensive preparation, and ability to demonstrate enthusiasm. To help save time, determine early on which industries to focus on. At the very least, you must know what the company does, who your interviewers are, what their seniority levels and backgrounds are, and what your duties will likely entail.

> For her in-house interview, Samantha investigated all the information she could find about the company, both through online resources and word of mouth. When her interviewer started telling her about the company structure, she gently interrupted him by saying, "Yes, and your company also does X, Y, and Z; it is involved in developing this new idea, and it is considering growing in this new area." The interviewer was dazzled by Samantha's level of preparation. Her in-depth knowledge and commendable enthusiasm earned her an offer.

Begin your preparation by reviewing Chapter 3 and consulting the sources discussed there. Additionally, rely on your headhunter. A good headhunter will make him- or herself available for mock interviews and will serve as an invaluable resource. Ideally, you should spend 30 to 60 minutes preparing with your headhunter for your in-house interview and review all the materials he or she gives you. If you have any contacts at the company or know people who have connections there, ask them for feedback as well. Finally, if you are interviewing with a public company, read their public filings to help you gain a better understanding of how it operates. You may be surprised to discover from public filings that the company is not doing so well.

> Shawn found out from his research that the company he was interested in was actually doing poorly. He explained: "When this happens, you better have a hell of a good reason to want to work there. Plus, the interviewers will want to know why you want to join a company that may be going down. They will wonder if you are not intelligent enough or simply too lazy to investigate."

Review the job description if there is one, but do not be surprised if your understanding of what the job entails turns out to be wrong. In-house attorneys often make a decision to hire someone before they actually figure out what that person's duties will be. After noticing changes in the market and meeting with candidates with diverse backgrounds, they may re-examine and redefine the job duties. Be flexible, and do not try to preemptively address the fact that you may lack certain experience. Let your interviewers be the judges of that. Nine out of 10 times, they will hire someone with a great personality over a slightly more qualified candidate. Moreover, they may view your lack of a particular experience as an opportunity to mentor you and to help you grow.

Personality Fit

In-house employers are concerned not only about your credentials and experience, but also about your versatility, good judgment, and cultural fit. You can usually get an offer from a firm even if one of the interviewers recommends against it, but this will not happen in-house. If a single in-house interviewer does not like you, this is a death knell for your future at the company. This is because in-house positions are more long-term, and in-house attorneys work very closely with each other on a daily basis. When they meet with you, the first question the attorneys will ask themselves is, "Can I go to lunch, travel, or have a beer with this person?" This is why it is so important to connect with your interviewers on a personal level and discuss common interests and hobbies.

Tuck away your sense of entitlement. Legal recruiters say that the biggest problem with qualified job applicants (who are otherwise strong candidates) is arrogance. Because they have excelled in all prior phases of their careers, they expect increasingly elite opportunities when it comes to in-house positions. If you think in-house employers would be lucky to have you, you will almost always fail. As one prominent recruiter (who frequently places candidates in the most coveted in-house positions) puts it, "Hundreds of Cravath-level lawyers are competing for a much smaller number of jobs. No matter how great you are, you are competing with five clones of you. So you better be damn enthusiastic about why you want this in-house position."

You cannot fake enthusiasm during an in-house interview. These people know they will have to work side by side with you for many years to come, and they are watching you very closely. If you really want to be successful, you must first convince *yourself* that you are truly excited about this opportunity. This should not be difficult—people can learn to get excited about even the most boring things (just think of an ERISA or tax lawyer who loves his or her job).

In short, treat this interview as a once-in-a-lifetime opportunity. Never allow an inflated sense of self-worth or outside distractions jeopardize your chances. Interview at the first available opportunity, and never cancel your interview once you have scheduled it, because you never know when and whether you will get another chance. This is true even under the most extenuating circumstances: Whether you are very ill or your case is going to trial, in-house employers may not be forgiving about a perceived lack of commitment.

Harvey had scheduled an interview for the in-house position of his dreams right before he was staffed on an important deal. Knowing he should not cancel the interview, Harvey showed up. Although he managed to give a great performance, he made a big mistake when he asked his interviewer if he could check his BlackBerry. Of course the interviewer agreed, but he called Harvey's recruiter shortly after the interview to inform him this was the only reason Harvey was not getting an offer. "If only he had excused himself to the bathroom and quietly checked his BlackBerry there, this would never be an issue," he said, obviously regretting losing such a great candidate.

Hours and Compensation

You should never discuss hours and compensation during an interview. This is true even for a cushy and relaxed in-house position. Negotiations with in-house employers are less challenging if you are working with a headhunter. A good headhunter will not only negotiate on your behalf, but he or she will also ask your employers the questions you may be unwilling to ask yourself.

The appropriate time to inquire about hours and compensation is after you get an offer, which is why you should not accept on the spot. By accepting too quickly, you are showing your desperation, as well as giving up an opportunity to investigate such important information as benefits, salary, and hours. Give yourself time to ask questions.

Christie, who made this mistake, advises against accepting right away. Although accepting on the spot demonstrated her strong interest in the job and helped her bond with her future colleagues, she regrets her hasty decision. When she accepted, the only information she had about the company was how much she would make. She did not ask for more money, she did not know what the vacation policy was, and she knew nothing about their health benefits. By accepting on the spot, Christie gave up a golden opportunity to negotiate.

The good news is that you will likely be informed about the possible range of your compensation and other relevant information, either through your headhunter or directly from your interviewers. If, for some reason, you cannot find out what the compensation range is, do not ask your interviewers before an offer. Instead, try to find out your market value by researching this information online, by asking your friends, or by inquiring with headhunters. Usually this will give you a ballpark idea of what to expect. If all else fails, assume that the compensation range is likely to be the same as or slightly less than what you are currently making. Companies are aware that many candidates experience a kind of reverse "sticker shock" when offered a salary that is significantly less than what they are currently making, so a range is given to prevent that. Additionally, remember that startup companies and "glamorous" in-house positions (in sports and entertainment, for example) usually pay less than hedge-fund positions, for example.

In-house salaries are eminently negotiable. Researching your market worth will help you answer questions about your salary expectations. Be realistic, as you can disqualify yourself by naming a number too high, or, conversely, hurt yourself by naming a number too low. Instead, armed with your research, give them the highest reasonable number and remember that it will likely be negotiated down somewhat. If your research yields nothing and you have no idea where to start, admit that you are not familiar with the range, wait for the employer to give you the range, and name a number slightly higher than that as a starting point. But if you are given a reasonable range, do not ask for more. Another possible approach is to ask, "Here is what I am making now—where does this fit in relation to the compensation you offer?" Alternatively, you can ask, "I understand that this job is not going to match my current compensation, and I am prepared to take a cut because this is what I want to do long-term. What is the range you are offering?"

Having Patience

In-house interviewing is a long, tedious process. It is also more random and less predictable than the process for firm interviewing. Your interviewers have obligations to the company, they have unexpected deadlines, and they often travel on short notice, so it is not uncommon for them to put the interviewing process on hold for weeks after having met you the first time. Be patient and do not try to pressure them into making you an offer quickly (unless you need to respond to another offer). Reiterate your interest every three weeks or so. Remember to write down your impressions about the interviewers and what was discussed. These notes will help you remember critical job-related information when deciding whether to accept an offer, and they will be handy when you start writing your thank-you letters. For in-house interviews, these letters are crucial. They can be brief, and you can e-mail rather than mail them. But do not be surprised if you do not hear anything back from them right away. Even if your interviewers liked you, they will be hesitant to establish a dialogue before a decision is made to hire you.

Asking the Right Questions

You do not want to be blindsided by what your assignments, hours, or compensation in-house actually end up being. This is why it is important to ask thoughtful questions. Although the more direct questions about lifestyle and compensation should be asked after you get an offer, you can ask more general questions about work environment, assignments, and benefits. Many candidates are so excited about an opportunity to work in-house that they will take it no matter what. Consequently, they pay little attention to any negative information they may have gleaned during their interviews. Ignore this kind of information at your peril! If they tell you, for example, "We will do our best to let you go home at 5 p.m., but there may be times when you have to stay later," investigate further. If you do not, you may be unpleasantly surprised with your hours after you start working there. Your interviewers will often hint at what will be expected of you, so pay attention to subtle cues.

> Lacey sought to leave her in-house position for one where she thought she would have better career advancement. During an interview, one of her interviewers said he was surprised at Lacey's interest in this job. Lacey could have brushed him off, but she carefully inquired further. She discovered that her new position would have a much more demanding schedule, the pay would be lower, and she would have fewer benefits. Learning this information helped Lacey decide this company was not a good fit for her after all.

Likewise, if personal reasons may preclude you from traveling or working late, be upfront with your employer (while emphasizing that you really want the job, of course). Your interviewers should know by the second or third round of interviews if something will be a dealbreaker for you. If you continue to interview after you are told about demanding hours or travel requirements, it is implied that you are agreeing to them.

For in-house interviews, your level of preparation and your personality are the two most important elements. Try to connect with your interviewers by talking about subjects such as hobbies or their achievements. Remember that it is always easier to click with your interviewers if you know something about them and show a genuine interest in working with them. If you exhibit excellent personal skills, if you are courteous and polite, and if you do not initiate discussions about hours and compensation before getting an offer, you are one step closer to getting that offer.

QuickReview

✓ Personality and preparedness are the keys to a successful in-house interview.

✓ Exhibit humility and show genuine interest in working with the company.

✓ Conduct thorough research about the company, your job requirements, and your interviewers.

✓ Never initiate a discussion about hours and compensation until the interviewer does.

✓ Be mindful of the interviewer's busy schedule, and be patient if a significant amount of time elapses between interviews.

✓ Record your impressions shortly after the interview, and always send thank-you letters.

✓ Do not ignore any negative information that could affect your decision to accept an offer.

Part V

Special Situations

Chapter 26

Tips for Using a Headhunter

⚜

Headhunters—also called recruiters—broker talent. They act as liaisons between law firms and attorneys, find out about openings, market candidates who may fit the profile, and help convince both parties they are a good match. Once the match is made, they receive hefty fees for their services (typically 25 to 35 percent of the candidate's base salary). Sounds easy enough. In reality, however, their jobs can be difficult and mundane. Headhunters spend days making cold calls, writing and responding to e-mails, following up with firms, and trying to drum up new leads.

How to Find a Headhunter

Usually, headhunters find you. If you have been practicing at a medium or large firm for a year or longer, you have probably received a number of phone calls, e-mails, and letters from headhunters. When deciding to make a move, most attorneys make a mistake by zeroing in on a headhunter who recently called them. This is not the best way to find a good headhunter! If you want the best of the best to represent you, you must do some homework. Start by asking your friends for recommendations, and rely heavily on word of mouth. Spend some time conducting your own research, too. The National Association of Legal Research Consultants is a good place to start. It lists reputable legal recruiting firms, which are required to comply with strict ethical guidelines. Also, if your credentials match the strict criteria of elite headhunting firms, you can ask them for help. Once you come up with some names, research them online. Aim for headhunters with a Website, good references, solid credentials, and prior firm experience. Check out their references, if possible. If any of these components are missing, proceed with caution.

What to look for

The following characteristics can help you distinguish between bad headhunters and good ones:

✓ Good headhunters provide honest feedback. They will tell you if you are applying too soon, if your desire to switch practice areas will hurt your chances, or if they cannot help you at all.

✓ Good headhunters are willing to help you prepare for an interview or answer questions even when it does not generate a fee.

✓ They spend at least 30 to 60 minutes preparing each candidate for an interview.

✓ They are responsive to your requests, questions, and concerns.

✓ They call you periodically, even when there is nothing to report.

✓ They try to meet you in person.

✓ They try to be available at the time convenient for you (provided you gave advance notice).

✓ Good headhunters, just like good lawyers, will acknowledge your inquiries and let you know when you can expect to hear from them.

✓ They show sincere interest in your career development.

✓ They serve as career counselors by helping you polish your resume and prepare for interviews, by advising you about your job prospects, and by providing you with helpful information about specific employers.

✓ They come highly recommended.

What to watch out for

Stay away from headhunters who do not have a Website and whose references do not check out. Beware of headhunters who are unresponsive or who promise you the stars but never deliver. There are some headhunters who will take your resume and promise you a job without ever intending to follow up. This behavior usually indicates that the headhunter does not have any leads and is simply keeping your application on file in case something comes along. Avoid the following kinds of headhunters, as well:

✓ Ones that try to match you with employers with bad reputations.

✓ Ones that target employers that do not meet your criteria.

✓ Ones that do not take the time to brainstorm options that may not generate a commission.

✓ Ones that do not reveal that you should contact certain employers yourself.

✓ Ones that push you into accepting without helping you figure out the pros and cons.

It is your responsibility to figure out whether to use a headhunter, whether to replace him or her, and when to be more proactive in your job search. If your headhunter is not being responsive, this is the first sign of trouble. And, of course, if it has been months, and the vague promises of jobs with top-ranked firms have not materialized, you should probably seek help elsewhere.

Who Can Use a Headhunter

For obvious reasons, headhunters do not represent candidates they do not think they can place. Generally, they work with candidates who have at least a year of firm experience. So you may not be able to work with a headhunter if your experience is limited to clerking, working for the government, working at a small firm, or working for less than a year. The key is to highlight a particular skill or experience that will make you an attractive candidate. Excellent work experience, publishing your work, and developing an expertise are all different ways to enhance your marketability. Make sure to mention these selling points to your headhunter when you first contact them.

Headhunters sometimes even turn down senior attorneys. This is because they do not want to put their reputation on the line with candidates who may not work out. So a partner who was de-equitized or a senior associate who was asked to leave his or her previous employer may have a harder time finding a reputable headhunter. As one recruiter says, "I would never work with candidates with a questionable past. I had a partner once ask me to help him move to a different firm. Excited about earning a six-figure referral fee, I did not do any homework about the partner. It was discovered later that the partner was fired from his former firm because he hired a female escort and billed it as a firm expense. I had put my reputation at stake by marketing him. I learned my lesson."

Sometimes, a headhunter may simply turn a candidate away because of the candidate's unreasonable demands or strong sense of entitlement. One respectable recruiting firm was rumored to have turned down a female partner after she commented, "Find out how much that job pays, because I am not commuting downtown for less than a million a year." Regardless of your level of seniority or experience, if a headhunter declines to work with you, do not be discouraged. Instead, ask him or her what you can do to make your candidacy more desirable, and take his or her feedback to heart. Then contact other legal recruiters to see if someone else may be interested in working with you. Mention that you would agree to representation even with the understanding that your chances are slim.

When to Use a Headhunter

Here are some situations in which using a headhunter might be helpful:

1. **If you are pressed for time.** The most important reason why lateral attorneys use headhunters is because of the tremendous amount of time and resources it takes to apply on their own. Let's face it—you cannot exactly ask your current employer to provide you with fancy resume paper and free mailing labels for your job search. You may also find it difficult to conduct a thorough job search and to go through the application process while you are billing hours at the office. Once you submit your resume to a headhunter, he/she does all the work for you. He/she is the one polishing your resume, making phone calls, writing e-mails, drafting cover letters, and following up with potential employers. He/she can also ensure that your job search is as thorough as possible. And he/she can help you make your move quickly. When you are applying on your own, it can take months before you receive any feedback about your applications. But with a headhunter's help, you can move in as little as three weeks.

2. **If you are relocating.** Michael Allen, a cofounder of Lateral Link, says using a headhunter is practically mandatory if you are moving to a new job market. This is especially true if you do not have a lot of free time on your hands. Headhunters will help you navigate through unfamiliar territory, educate you on market-specific cultural differences, and offer their regional knowledge to help with your job search. Furthermore, they will help you ensure that your interviewing schedule in the new market is neatly packed into one or two trips, rather than the multiple trips you may face if applying on your own.

3. **If you have questions or need someone with connections.** Good headhunters are resourceful. They hold your hand throughout the process, answer your questions about the firm, and address your concerns. They also serve as a liaison between you and the firm, and give the firm an opportunity to ask you questions it would not be able to ask otherwise. And, if they are really good, they will be on a first-name basis with the recruiting coordinators, so their submissions receive priority attention. They also have good connections and a solid reputation in the legal community. Many headhunters are known for working only with those candidates who have strong credentials or who are otherwise a perfect match for the advertised positions. These headhunters can vouch for their candidates, as they always verify resumes for accuracy. So employers commonly rely on these headhunters to do their screening for them, and they view submissions from these headhunters as more credible.

4. **If you need extra cash.** Some recruiting companies now offer an added incentive for lateral candidates. If you work with their headhunters, you can receive a placement bonus after you accept an offer you secured with the headhunter's help. For some, especially for junior candidates burdened with student loans, this bonus can be a huge incentive.

5. **If you need to up your negotiating power.** Headhunters can help you gain greater bargaining power with legal employers. Although you should always try to negotiate with your employer about things that are important to you, headhunters are always in a much better position to negotiate with the employer on your behalf. They know how to use your offer from one potential employer as leverage in negotiations with others. They can also help you raise the issues with the employer you may be reluctant to raise on your own. Finally, they can ask sensitive financial questions that you cannot. For instance, if you want to inquire about a signing bonus or an extra year of credit, or ask the firm to match incentives offered by another firm, it is easier to have the headhunter do the talking. That way, you do not risk coming off as greedy—it is just the headhunter doing his or her job.

When Not to Use a Headhunter

There are some not-so-obvious disadvantages to working with a headhunter. For starters, headhunters do not always have your best interests in mind. Driven by the incentive to collect their fee, they may push you into accepting an offer from an employer that is not your ideal fit. Additionally, headhunters charge firms substantial fees, and this can make it more difficult for you to land your dream job. For example, when presented with two equally qualified candidates, the firm may choose the one who did not use a headhunter in order to save on the hiring expenses. In fact, certain firms may not interview any candidates who apply through headhunters. This is especially true for smaller, regional firms and for candidates with little work experience. Moreover, employers who are flooded with qualified applicants do not have the need to shell out headhunter fees.

Finally, you may have to forgo a headhunter if you are hoping to receive a significant signing bonus or reimbursement of your debt to the old firm. In some cases, employers are more reluctant to sweeten the pot if it costs them money to hire you. Therefore, depending on your job preferences, you should weigh your options carefully.

Arianna, who was looking to make a lateral move as a third-year associate, retained an elite recruiting firm to help her with her search. Even though she practiced in a large city, there were only eight firms to which she could apply, due to the nature of her practice and her desire to work at a large firm. Fortunately for Arianna, she had excellent credentials. Even so, because of the limited number of options, she decided to apply to three law firms on her own and to the other five using a headhunter. She ended up with invitations to interview at the three firms where she applied by herself. The other five firms that were approached via a headhunter either declined to interview her or indicated they would keep her resume on file "in case something came up." Notably, because there was an economic slowdown that year, it was a bad year to be making a move. The five firms to which Arianna applied with the head-hunter would have hired her, but they were discouraged from interviewing her due to the added expense of the headhunter's fee.

When in Doubt

If you are unsure whether you should work with a headhunter, consider splitting your duties. Ask the headhunter to approach certain firms, indicating that you will apply to other firms yourself. This way, if the headhunter's fee turns out to be a discouragement for some firms, you will still have other opportunities available to you at the firms where you applied on your own. Furthermore, a headhunter may be willing to reduce their fee for cost-sensitive firms, so remember to ask if that is an option.

Another important tip to keep in mind is that you should never work with more than one headhunter in the same geographical area. Inevitably, they will end up submitting your applications to the same employers, creating confusion and making you appear unprofessional. The only time you should use two headhunters for your search is when you are applying in two different locations or industries and want to work with head-hunters who know the intricacies of these areas. And even then, be sure to inform them about their mutual existence to help avoid duplicate submissions.

Finally, in some circumstances, you may find that an internal referral by someone who knows you and who already works at your dream firm may work much better for you than a referral from a headhunter. However, make sure that your reference has a solid reputation at the firm. If you are in doubt regarding his or her reputation, only use this person as an information resource, and submit an application on your own.

If you decide to move, headhunters—especially good ones—can make your life a lot easier. Before you retain a headhunter, however, consider your particular circumstances and market conditions. Make certain that the headhunter's fee will not deter employers from hiring you. If you work with a headhunter, ask him or her to lay out a realistic career trajectory for you, and do your own research to ensure you are getting the whole picture. Finally, make sure that your headhunter keeps in touch with you and does not put your career goals on the back burner. Remember, a headhunter can be a great resource, but, ultimately, you are responsible for your own career.

QuickReview

✓ Typically, candidates with at least one year of law firm experience can use headhunters.

✓ Share your key selling points during your first conversation with a headhunter to ensure that he/she gets the full picture.

✓ Do not rely on cold-calling when choosing a headhunter; do your own homework and check references.

✓ Pros: They act as gatekeepers for the firm, possessing all the inside information about openings and ensuring that your resume gets noticed. It is also much easier to make a move with the help of a headhunter than it is doing it on your own.

✓ Cons: Their work is fee-driven, and they may attempt to influence your choice for the sake of making a placement. Some firms may also pass on your candidacy because of headhunter fees.

✓ If you are not getting enough attention or feedback from your headhunter, start looking for a different one or apply on your own.

Chapter 27

INTERVIEWING IN A BAD ECONOMY OR AFTER GETTING FIRED

❦

Whether you are interviewing because you were let go or because you are seeking new opportunities, the rules are different in an economic downturn. This is not the time to exhibit a sense of entitlement or desperation, nor is it the time to be unprepared. Be ready to discuss why you are interviewing, but do not volunteer negative information without being asked. Preparation, good answers to difficult questions, and a positive attitude are the keys to getting an offer in a bad economy.

Job Hunting in a Bad Economy

If you already have a job and there is a good chance you can keep it, it may be better to hold off on interviewing until the economy improves. There is always a risk that your current employer will find out and fire you for looking elsewhere. On the flipside, if you know you are going to be laid off, interview as soon as possible. It is much easier to find a job if you are still employed. If there is a gap on your resume, make sure you convince interviewers that your legal skills are up to par. Explain what you are doing to keep up with the industry, such as writing articles, volunteering, attending networking events, or taking CLE classes.

If you are currently out of work, your interviewers may want to call your former supervisors for references. Contact them ahead of time and casually inquire as to what they will say; it is important to anticipate negative feedback and tell the interviewers a consistent story. Always ask your former supervisors for the best possible reference they can give you. Try to pick people who like you or who are at least sympathetic to your position. If you suspect they will mention negative information about you, remind them about your solid work product and any positive evaluations they gave you, then ask them to be generous with their feedback.

Finally, think carefully before asking a recruiter to help with your move. Many firms are reluctant to pay headhunter fees during an economic downturn when they already receive hundreds of applications from over-qualified job seekers. But a good headhunter may have connections and thus know about unadvertised openings. They can also help package your application to make it stand out. Read Chapter 26 and research this issue before deciding.

To Tell or Not to Tell

If you lost your job, you must first decide whether to disclose this to potential employers. If you were publicly fired and/or others know about your layoff, you have no choice. But if your employer is quietly letting you interview while keeping you on the payroll and allowing office access, you may be able to change jobs before your job status officially changes to "unemployed."

In deciding whether to tell, first evaluate your situation. What was the reason for your departure? If you and 20 other associates from a structured finance group were told to look for other employment opportunities because of the credit crunch, disclosing this fact to potential employers is unlikely to jeopardize your job search. If anything, it may evoke sympathy. On the other hand, if you were fired because of a conflict with a partner or because of performance-related issues, you may not want to volunteer that information. In a bad economy, it may make getting a legal job impossible. However, you cannot lie or misrepresent the true reasons why you left.

> After missing a major deadline, Noelle was told to look for a new job. But when potential employers asked her about her current job status, she lied and told them she was on a partnership track but wanted a more challenging position. When the true reasons for her departure came out, her offers were withdrawn, and her reputation was irretrievably damaged.

Do not be dishonest, but do not volunteer negative information either. If your employer encourages you to interview "quietly," take advantage of this opportunity. But if you decide to be forthcoming, you must give the interviewers solid reasons for them to take a chance on you. Explain what qualities make you a strong candidate and why your termination has no bearing on your ability to succeed.

Getting Laid Off

Never mistakenly say you were fired. There is a big difference between being fired and being laid off. People are usually fired for poor performance but laid off for economic reasons. Employers are less likely to take a chance on the former. Of course, this line is blurred by the firms that blame mass layoffs on performance issues, but most other firms can see right through this. If you decide to address the fact that you were laid off, make sure you qualify this statement with an explanation. The more specific you are, the more convincing you will be. For example:

✓ "My firm had two rounds of layoffs in the last six months. I survived the first round, but 45 people lost their jobs. During the second round, when I was laid off, the firm laid off 30 more people."

✓ "The reason the firm had to let me and the others go is because it lost six major clients on whose matters I was working full-time."

✓ "My former employer had to cut 30 percent of its workforce."

✓ "I was one of 28 associates in my department who lost their jobs due to the bad economy."

You can further alleviate concerns about your candidacy by proactively discussing your strengths and outstanding performance.

> Ken received an offer after being laid off because he showed he was an asset as a lawyer. He emphasized the positive feedback and the level of responsibility he received at his previous job. Additionally, he mentioned that several of his former bosses and clients offered to serve as his references. Finally, he pulled out copies of evaluations and complimentary e-mails from partners and clients. This was enough to convince his interviewers he deserved a shot.

Getting Fired

If you were fired, do not despair. It happens to some of the best people in the profession. Just think of the recently dismissed U.S. attorneys. Take a deep breath and exhale. Now put all those bad thoughts behind you, because now is the time to figure out what is next.

You should know at the outset that the legal job market is not very forgiving of people who were fired, especially those fired for performance-related reasons. Thus, if you decide to keep this fact to yourself, make sure that you do not tell anyone about your misfortune. When asked by your peers why you are no longer working for your employer, explain that you are taking time off, or that you quit, or that you got burned out and decided to do something else for a while. To ensure you do not have a significant gap in employment—a potential red flag on your resume—start interviewing immediately. And try to line up a law-related gig as soon as possible, regardless of what it entails.

Unless they suspect something, potential employers are not likely to ask you whether you were fired. Most likely they will simply ask why you want to work for them. Again, you should not be dishonest, but do not disclose more than you have to. Focus on positive factors (your desire for more responsibility, the new firm's reputation, the type of work you want to do, and so on). You can also explain that your prior employer does not have a certain practice group or that you want to work in a different location; once you really think about this, you can find many genuine reasons for wanting a change.

Finally, if you must disclose that you were fired, be upfront about the reason, but phrase your answer in a way that emphasizes that it was an isolated incident, that it will not happen again, and that you have learned from it. Keep it brief and do not sound apologetic. Follow it up with positive examples of your solid work performance and good evaluations.

Never Criticize Former Employers

Losing a job is devastating, and you may be tempted to speak ill of those who caused your misfortune. No matter how angry you are, however, never say anything bad about your former employer. It is unprofessional, and it will almost certainly cost you an offer. Do not sound like a victim, and do not be negative, sarcastic, desperate, or bitter. Put hurt feelings behind you and focus on the positive. How do you do this? Realize that the most successful candidates always say a few positive things about their former employer and then explain why the new employer is a better fit.

If you are interviewing in a bad economy, three simple steps can help you succeed. First, always stay positive when discussing your job experience, reasons for interviewing, former employers, and so on. Second, be armed with good evaluations, solid references, and positive feedback from former employers or clients. Finally, be honest, but do not volunteer negative information without being asked. It is not impossible to obtain a job in bad economy—you just may have to work harder for it.

QuickReview

✓   If an employer gives you an opportunity to remain on their payroll while interviewing, take them up on the offer.

✓   Do not delay your job search if your current job is at risk; interview with as many employers as possible.

✓   If you were let go, figure out whether and how to address this subject during interviews.

✓   Always offer good reasons for wanting to make a move, which should have nothing to do with your needing a job.

✓   Make sure your reasons for interviewing and your description of your past job performance are consistent with what your former employer will say.

✓   If you have gaps on your resume or if you never had a legal job before, tell your employer how you are keeping up your legal skills.

✓   Never badmouth a former employer, and always be positive and upbeat.

Chapter 28

Dealing With Rejection

∾✖∾

Anyone casting a broad net in a job search is bound to receive at least a few rejection letters. And of course, if you are applying for legal jobs everywhere, the stack of rejection letters you receive may be rather large. Most rejection letters will dispose of your associate dreams with ruthless efficiency. We recently saw one that was one sentence long. It read: "We have reviewed your application, and we are not in a position to pursue your candidacy further." Apparently the recipient of this letter was rather surprised to receive it, but not because of its brevity. As it turns out, he had never actually applied to the firm. Some firms take "efficiency" to the next level, sending mass rejections via e-mail, and listing the names of all rejected candidates in the "To" field. A word of caution: No matter how tempted you may be to feed a thin envelope into the shredder, open it first. Strangely enough, some employers still send out callback invitations in the mail, and these letters can be thin enough to be mistaken for a rejection.

Do Not Read Too Much Into It

Whether you got rejected after sending out your resume, after interviewing on campus, or after attending a full-blown callback or lateral interview, do not take the rejection personally. A rejection does not necessarily mean that your credentials or your interviewing style are sub par. It could simply mean someone else's credentials are better, or that the spot has already been filled, or that the firm does not need an attorney with your level of experience right now. This by no means rules out your candidacy with them in the future. Employers often reject a candidate only to hire the same person at a later time.

The sobering fact is that most resume submissions are headed for the same place—the recycling bin. Law firms receive so many submissions that it is simply impossible for them to consider every application. On most days, a firm's recruiting department will receive at least a dozen applications. Your application will only make it to the hiring partner's desk if there is an urgent need for someone with your qualifications or if your credentials are outstanding. This means it is unlikely that the person with the hiring power will even see your resume.

Keep in mind that many employers interview more candidates than they need, hoping to have a better pool of candidates or expecting that only a small number will accept. Some employers even conduct interviews when they have no vacancies. One small firm recently interviewed three lateral candidates. All three had stellar credentials, were great interviewees, and were recommended by their interviewers for offers. Problem was, there was just one opening. The hiring partner decided that the candidates would be given offers in the order they were interviewed. Thus, the first candidate would be given an offer first; if she declined, an offer would be given to the second candidate, and so on. The first candidate in this case declined the offer, but candidate number two accepted (unfortunately for candidate number three). Moral of the story: An excellent candidate can be passed over simply because of a scheduling issue.

It's a Small World

Being rejected is a very unpleasant experience, especially if you have invested a great deal of time and effort into the application and interviewing process. A candidate we know underwent a tedious application process, filled out lengthy questionnaires, wrote essays, attended day-long interviews, and then waited for six months to learn of her rejection from the U.S. Attorney's Office. Undoubtedly a frustrating experience. However, as upset as you may be, remember to maintain a professional demeanor, even (or especially) with the employers that rejected you. In this candidate's case, she sent a polite thank-you letter to her interviewers, and when she interviewed with them again a year later, she got the job.

The legal profession is like small-town politics—everybody knows everybody. This is true even for BigLaw firms and large legal markets. For example, the partners from the New York firm that rejected you may know partners from another firm you are applying to. People talk, and there is a good chance you may run into the person who signed your rejection letter. In fact, you should assume it will happen and let that assumption guide all your interactions with potential employers. Be courteous and professional, do not exhibit bitterness or ill will, and remind yourself that they are big fish in your tank, and there is no reason to upset the big fish needlessly.

Kelly once interviewed with his dream law firm. Although the interview went well, the firm's hiring partner, Bruce, later called Kelly to tell him he did not get an offer.

Kelly was extremely disappointed; hoping for another chance, he accepted a clerkship position instead. One year later, while clerking for a judge, Kelly received a call about a case on the judge's docket. The caller asked apologetically about the judge's policy on accepting late motions. Kelly recognized Bruce's voice and was initially tempted to give Bruce a hard time. But his better judgment told him to be polite and courteous to Bruce. Smartly, Kelly realized their paths would likely cross again. Kelly was right. Two years later, when the firm had an opening, Kelly was offered a position there.

The moral of the story is even more apparent when applied to small legal markets or clerkship interviews. In a small town, the prospect of running into the same lawyer at some point in your career is almost certain. Although the prospect of having a case before the same judge who interviewed you largely depends on geography, keep in mind that judges (both state and federal) talk amongst themselves. Federal judges in particular have a very tight membership club. Always be courteous to all of your interviewers, including those who have rejected you. In fact, consider sending a thank-you letter to the person who rejected you after a callback interview. Thank the interviewer for taking the time to meet with you, express your regrets about not getting an offer, and indicate an interest in being considered for future openings. In the long run, such a letter may serve you well and may be just enough to convince your dream employer to reconsider your application the next time there is an opening.

Seek Feedback

Use your rejection as a learning opportunity and a chance to improve your interviewing skills. Send an e-mail to one or two of the interviewers, asking them for feedback. Or ask your headhunter to inquire on your behalf. Sometimes you will get a generic response from interviewers who are afraid to reveal the real reasons for your rejection, but some interviewers are more forthcoming, so it is worth a shot. Just remember to stay positive, do not get defensive or accusatory, and keep your inquiry brief. This is not the same as confronting your ex about why he or she dumped you; if you want a response, you must approach your interviewers in a much more delicate manner. Consider the following inquiry:

"Thank you very much for taking the time to interview me. I thoroughly enjoyed meeting you and your colleagues and was disappointed to learn I will not be joining you. I really hope you can provide me with some feedback on what I could have done better. As a young lawyer, I strive to develop good interpersonal, communication, and interviewing skills. If you could share some general feedback or offer advice on how I could hone my interviewing skills, I would be extremely grateful. Thank you in advance for taking the time to get back to me, either by e-mail or telephone, whichever you are most comfortable with. And again, I appreciated the opportunity to interview."

No one likes being rejected. But you should get over your fear and dislike of rejection letters, as they are bound to happen, and try not to take them personally. There are any number of reasons (unrelated to your candidacy) why you may not have been given an offer. No matter how unhappy you are about the bad news, accept the rejection gracefully. Your tact and professionalism, especially in a tight legal community, will serve you well for years to come. Finally, seek feedback from the interviewers who rejected you on what you could have done better. This may help you hone your interviewing skills for future interviews.

QuickReview

✓ Remember, employers send out rejections for a variety of reasons, some of which may have nothing to do with you personally.

✓ Do not get discouraged and do not react negatively to the bad news.

✓ Know that a rejection does not forever prevent you from working for this employer.

✓ Consider sending a thank-you letter to the interviewer(s) who rejected you—it may help your candidacy in the future.

✓ Also consider seeking feedback about your interviewing skills.

Chapter 29

NEGOTIATING AN OFFER

❧⚬⚬❧

You have an offer. Congratulations! You must be feeling excited, energized, and anxious all at the same time. Our job is to help you do away with the anxious part. Let us start by revealing the two most important secrets of legal interviewing: First, never accept an offer on the spot. Second, negotiate before sealing the deal. This is true for all legal jobs, but the advice is especially pertinent if you are considering a position in a firm.

Never Accept on the Spot

Regardless of what anyone else says, you would be a fool to accept an offer on the spot. You may hear stories about candidates who accepted on the spot, but these stories are not in praise of the candidates' decisiveness—they are a pat on the back for the firm. Their only purpose is to brag about (1) how in control the interviewers were, and (2) how great the firm is that people feel compelled to accept on the spot. Unfortunately, if you are one of those candidates who accept an offer as soon as they receive it, you will probably acquire a reputation for being a pushover or a yes-man.

As you are reading this advice, you may be thinking to yourself, *But this is the only offer I can get/ this is my dream job/I am so grateful for this opportunity—I simply must accept on the spot.* Our advice remains the same. The firm does not know that they are your only option or your top choice. They are also not going to withdraw their offer if you do not accept right off the bat. Therefore, you will not lose anything by putting them off. By accepting on the spot, you are (1) communicating to them that you did not have any other/better options, and (2) giving up an opportunity to negotiate. Even if you think you may have nothing to negotiate, some issues may come up once you give them some thought.

Negotiate Before Accepting

It may be tempting to accept on the spot and do away with all the uncertainty regarding your future and all the anxiety attendant to the hiring process. However, before you accept an offer, you should figure out if there are any issues you would like to address with your future employer. Take your time, ask questions, get to know the firm, and let them woo you into working for them. This pre-commitment, "dating" stage of your relationship is the best time in your career to ask questions and to negotiate. In fact, you will not have another chance to bargain over your rights and privileges with the firm until after you make partner and have the leverage of important clients.

The biggest misconception we had as law students was that a firm would always be afraid to lose us and that we would retain that same bargaining power once we joined. Nothing could be further from the truth. In fact, both our own experience and surveys of associates at various firms across the country reveal that the majority of firms are only willing to negotiate with attorneys and students *before* they accept. After you start working for a firm, you will find yourself in a fairly powerless position. Unfortunately, this is the way things work. Perhaps high associate attrition rates have something to do with this; firms may not want to invest much in their associates, knowing that most of them will leave within a few years anyway. Another reason for this is competitive salaries. Employers who pay you a high salary may not feel the need to accommodate you further. You work, and they pay you and give you experience. In their view, that is enough.

Finally, if you are interviewing with the firms while still in law school, NALP surveys and on-campus rumors can have a significant impact on a firm's image. These factors give you more bargaining power than you will ever have later in your career. Once you are hired, you can no longer give negative feedback about the firm, and consequently the firm does not have to keep accommodating your requests. Although publications such as the *National Law Journal* feature associate satisfaction surveys, they have minimal impact. So, the bottom line is, negotiate before accepting an offer!

Start Dates

One issue up for negotiation is your start date. If you are a law student interviewing for a summer position, you may be interested in moving your start or end date. For example, you may want to ask the firm about starting at a different time than the rest of the summer class because you want to split your summer between two firms. Or you may be interested in moving your start or end date due to a planned vacation. Or you may simply want to start earlier or work longer because you need the money. Whatever your reason is, you should raise this issue before you accept an offer. Be prepared to hear "no," however, because more and more firms are becoming less flexible, especially as the economy is taking a downturn. Most firms, especially large ones, will require you to start and end at the same time the rest of the summer associates do. But many firms still allow flexibility. Those who do not ask do not receive, so definitely ask!

If you plan to join a firm as a first-year associate, your biggest concern regarding timing will be your start date. Some first-years who really need the money want to start as soon as they are done with the bar exam. Others want to take three months off to travel the world. One thing you should know is that the longer you wait to ask for changes, and the closer it is to your scheduled start date, the less likely you are to get what you want. If possible, ask a year in advance. Here is why: The NALP provides statistics about each firm's summer associate/incoming associate acceptance rates. Firms want to look good and receive top rankings, and a high acceptance rate for permanent employment makes them look good. If your request precedes your acceptance, a firm may be willing to bend over backward and accommodate it. Keep this in mind as you are making your plans for the year.

Find out what the impact of your start date will be on your year-end bonus. At most firms outside of New York, you will not receive a year-end bonus if you miss the cutoff date; however, a number of firms do pay prorated bonuses to first-year associates who start working *before* the cutoff date. Most often, the cutoff date to be eligible for a bonus is in August or September. Therefore, if you manage to negotiate an early start date, you may be one of only few associates in your class who will actually receive a bonus that year.

Charlotte accepted a job at a BigLaw firm. Before she accepted, she asked the firm to allow her to start in mid-August. She ended up being the only first-year associate among 100 to get a bonus that year. Everyone else started after the cutoff date of August 31. Her clever strategy made her $10,000 richer that year.

Finally, if you are a lateral attorney and you are interviewing at the end of the year, you may want to stay with your old firm until you receive your bonus. Or you may want to start at the new firm early in the year so you can bill more hours and not have to go too long without a paycheck. Or perhaps you will want to take some time off in between jobs to enjoy a nice, guilt-free vacation. Everyone knows that will not happen once you start (certainly, not without guilt anyway!). All these things are possible and negotiable.

One reason a firm may not be accommodating of your request is if you were made an offer because they were slammed with work. In this case, they will expect you to start as soon as possible, and there will not be much room to negotiate your start date. But other perks may be up for grabs.

> Anya, who recently lateraled to a new firm, was "strongly encouraged" to start ASAP. When she attempted to nego- tiate a later start date, the firm politely reminded her that she knew when she interviewed that they needed her to start right away. Even though she could not negotiate a later date, she was able to get something in return before she finally ac- cepted. Because she really needed a vacation, she convinced the firm to allow her to take a month-long vacation later in the year.

You may also ask your new employer to make up for a bonus you are losing by leaving your old firm too soon.

Summer Splits

Splitting the summer between two legal jobs is something every law student should seriously consider. You will not have another opportunity like this in your career to figure out what works for you.

> Jacob split his 1L summer between a mid-sized firm and a small firm. He then split his 2L summer between two large firms in different cities. Finally, he did an externship for legal services during his 1L year and for a judge during his 2L year. Jacob learned a great deal from these experiences. First, he discovered he did not really want to clerk or work for the gov- ernment. An excellent and hardworking student, he received of- fers from all four firms. His experience at the two large firms taught him that his personality was not suited for a large-firm environ- ment. He liked working at a place where he could know every- one by name. However, his summer experience also showed him the drawbacks of being in a firm that was too small—there was too much control over face time and associate schedule, and anyone could get fired on a whim. Therefore, he chose a mid- sized firm, where he has been happily practicing ever since.

Splitting the summer not only gives you more exposure to different firms, but it also allows you to explore different kinds of work assignments— and, hopefully, receive multiple job offers. Accordingly, we cannot em- phasize strongly enough that you should consider pursuing this option if you can. Although more and more large firms discourage splitting, you can still negotiate with many of them, as they all can make exceptions if they really want you. If you decide to take this route, you should always try to approach a senior partner with this request, preferably the one who you feel really likes you and will stand up for you. Associates, even senior associates, do not have the power to make exceptions. So, approach a partner who you think has a great deal of pull. Try to make this request early in the fall. Toward the end of the hiring season (November through December), larger firms often end up with too many acceptances, and they secretly hope some of the candidates with pending offers will not accept. On the other hand, in September, firms are still very anxious, even worried, that they are not getting enough acceptances from good students. This makes early fall the best time to "trade in" your acceptance for an opportunity to split.

Some firms may allow you to split a summer between two offices at the same firm. This is better than not splitting at all, because at least you will be exposed to two different locations and work environments. But beware—some firms will not give you an offer if only one office supports it. So, even if the New York partners really like you, you may not get an offer if their Dallas partners decide to pass on your candidacy. Furthermore, city splits can indicate geographic indecisiveness, and the firm may choose to pass on your request in hopes of giving your spot to another candidate who has stronger ties to the area.

Part-Time Work During the School Year

If you are really lucky, you may be able to negotiate an opportunity to work part-time at your law firm during the school year. This option is usually only available to students going to law school in cities where the firm has an office. An opportunity to make money during law school is a major selling point for some New York and D.C. firms, which lure summer associates into accepting permanent offers with promises of lucrative, part-time employment. Associates who accept solely for this reason, however, sometimes complain later on that it was an empty promise. Some firms give you work for a few weeks or a couple of months after you accept and then brush you off, explaining that they are "really slow." So, do not put too much stock in this perk when making your decision. On the other hand, if you are inclined to accept with the firm anyway, asking about part-time work never hurts. Even a few weeks of law-firm pay means that you will be several thousand dollars ahead of the game while still in law school.

Clerkships

If you are interviewing for a clerkship, you may want to discuss this with your firm before you accept their offer. Some firms may not allow you to clerk unless you have negotiated or reserved that option prior to accepting an offer from them. Because letting your firm know about your clerkship is a delicate question, try to do it as tactfully and as early as possible. Conversely, many judges will not allow you to accept an offer from a firm while you are clerking. So it is a good idea to know everyone's policy on this issue.

Signing Bonus

Attorneys usually do not negotiate their bonuses, but there are some exceptions. First, if you are coming to a firm after a clerkship, some firms are amenable to negotiating the amount of your clerkship bonus, including whether to give an additional bonus and/or seniority credit for a two-year clerkship, and whether to pay for your bar and moving expenses. Second, if you happen to be at the right place at the right time (for example, during an IP boom in Southern California) and if you have the right background (in this case, a technical degree), a firm will happily give you a signing bonus to join a busy practice. Some firms will also give you a bonus if you choose to summer with them during the first part of the summer. Third, if you are making a lateral move, you may be able to receive a signing bonus if you make the move as soon as the firm requests. This happens when the firm's practice is very busy and they desperately need more associates to cover the work. In this case, they will often happily shell out tens of thousands of dollars in a signing bonus, and/or agree to make up for the year-end bonus you lost by leaving the old firm. Fourth, if you are interviewing for in-house positions, you can usually negotiate your salary after you get an offer. Be sure to read Chapter 25 for advice on how to negotiate for a salary within or above a given salary range. Finally, if you are working with a headhunter, ask him or her to help in negotiations with your future employer. Legal recruiters are in a much better position to negotiate with a firm, especially when it comes to such sensitive issues as money. Moreover, he/she will likely know which firms are open to this subject and which are not.

Expenses and Costs

At most large firms, what you receive for your bar and moving expenses is non-negotiable. These firms have established uniform policies that apply in all or most of their offices, and delineate precisely which expenses are covered and which are not. However, with smaller or mid-sized firms, there may be room for negotiation. For example, if the firm offers to pay for moving your furniture but not your car, you can convince them to give you a check instead and budget your move accordingly. Or, if they voice a strong desire to hire you, you may convince them to pick up your bar costs by letting them know that another firm offered this. As always, it never hurts to ask.

Work Assignments

This section is crucial if you are joining a firm with the intention of working in a certain department or group, or being assigned to certain types of cases or transactions. So review the job description carefully (unless your firm is very small or it requires junior associates to rotate through all the groups). As more senior attorneys will tell you, negotiating work assignments is one of the most important topics to address before accepting an offer. Here is why: If you have preconceived notions about what kind of work you want to do and with whom you want to work, always ask about this before accepting an offer. You can inquire whether you will be able to work on certain cases, whether you will receive assignments from particular partners, whether you can request a mentor of your choice, and whether you can be certain you will work in a particular practice area. Most of the time, if the firm promises to honor your request, it will be honored.

Working at a law firm, big or small, is a lot about luck. You may get lucky and receive work from great partners who treat you well, who do not bother you much on weekends, and who give you challenging assignments. Or you may get stuck working with a partner who calls you on Sunday morning and asks you to come to the office to help him find a pleading on his desk. You may get to take depositions during your first few months at the firm, or you may get pigeonholed into doing document review for two years. When you start at a firm, there is only so much you can do to increase your odds. But before you start, you can definitely improve your chances of working for the right partners and on the right cases by asking the firm to promise you those things. Later, when you are prepping for a deposition while your next-door neighbor is losing his mind over a 100-hour document review project, you will be glad you did. When you do ask the firm to make these promises to you, however, remember that they are not set in stone. To improve your chances, make your requests in writing. Keep records, and forward these records to the firm as a reminder a few weeks before you start. This way, the firm will have every reason to accommodate your requests.

A job offer gives you a chance to put on your lawyer hat and negotiate like a lawyer. This may be the only time in your early career when you have this kind of bargaining power. Have no qualms about asking for what is important to you. Remember, you are not asking for favors—you are negotiating, the same way you would negotiate a deal or a settlement on behalf of a client. That said, do not feel entitled, and approach the firm as gently, politely, and deferentially as you can. Even if the answer is no, it is better to know about it before you accept. Knowledge can help you evaluate your options, so shop your offer around, negotiate with other firms, and make an informed decision about where you want to work. For example, if you discover that certain policies are set in stone, you will still have time to decide whether to give up certain perks in exchange for what will hopefully be a satisfying career.

QuickReview

✓ Never accept an offer on the spot. Once you accept, you give up all of your bargaining power.

✓ Start dates can be important for a variety of reasons and are often negotiable.

✓ If you are interviewing as a lateral, you can often negotiate your start date in light of any signing bonuses or year-end bonuses you gave up by leaving your old firm.

✓ Depending on the firm and the legal market, summer splits may be an option.

✓ Remember to ask the firm about work projects and departmental assignments before accepting.

✓ Try to get the firm to promise that you will work with certain attorneys or on certain types of cases.

✓ Do not be arrogant, but do not undersell yourself.

Chapter 30

Unique Challenges for Foreign Applicants

Being invited to interview with a U.S. employer usually means they have accepted your background and credentials. Therefore, your priority is to convince them you want to work and stay in a certain geographical area long-term. Because not every interviewer is familiar with the educational and legal systems in your country of origin, be prepared to explain what your work experience and credentials mean. At the interview stage, most employers will not ask about your immigration status, and you should not initiate discussions about visas.

Ties to the Area

Employers are reluctant to hire and train lawyers who will not stay with them long term. This applies to both American lawyers and those born outside the United States. When interviewing for a job in a particular geographical area, you must demonstrate a commitment to staying in that area. For applicants born outside the United States, this is even more important. Employers may ask you a variety of "why" questions—why you want to stay in this area, why you want to practice in the United States, why you want to work for them. All these questions serve one goal: to investigate whether you plan to commit to working for them for the long haul.

When Peter was interviewing with a large New York firm, he was asked repeatedly about his ties to the area. One of the partners was especially adamant about this question. Not convinced that Peter could hack it in the big city, he leaned back in his chair, looked at Peter with a hint of disapproval, and said, "I am a native New Yorker, my grandfather was a New Yorker, my great-grandfather was a New Yorker, and I have lived here my entire life. Why do you want to come here?" Peter looked into the interviewer's eyes and answered with sincerity, "Because I want my children to be native New Yorkers." The interviewer was genuinely pleased with this answer.

If you want the job, you must show real commitment and a desire to stay. Do not show ambivalence when answering the "why" questions. If you waffle and say you plan to work here for a year or two, you will likely not get an offer. You must be able to explain why you want to leave your home country, work in the States, move to a certain geographical area, and work for this particular employer. If you have ties to the area, bring them up. For example, if your relatives or a significant other live there, or if you went to school there, employers will find it more believable that you want to work and stay in that area. Some candidates also find it helpful to mention that they have already permanently relocated to the United States, made friends here, adjusted to the area, and hope to get a job here and stay long term.

If you do not have any connections to the area, discuss why you feel comfortable there. If you are interviewing in New York, for example, you can say that your commitment to a particular practice area makes it essential that you work in a major world financial market. To this end, you can discuss your relevant work experience, commitment to building a certain expertise, and language skills. Just remember to conduct research ahead of time and discuss the areas of law that are relevant to what the firm does. It is also advantageous to take the bar in your desired geographic area before applying for jobs there. Because bar admissions requirements for foreign attorneys vary from state to state, this will also help you figure out whether you are eligible to practice in the state where you hope to land a job.

Finally, if the interviewer mentions the firm's desire to open an office in your home country, show eagerness to help get the office up and running. In these circumstances, the firm is likely more interested in your ability to be a team player than it is in your commitment to remain in the United States. Once you get your foot in the door, you can always negotiate a deal in which you would be able to move back to the States later. Meanwhile, the firm will appreciate your willingness to commit to their long-term growth.

Emphasize Your Experience and Skills

Be prepared to explain your experience, education, and skills. Explain exactly what you have done, what you have learned, what you are good at, and why this makes you a strong candidate. U.S. employers are very receptive to hiring foreign lawyers who can offer a unique perspective, practical skills, or an ability to interact with foreign clients. Point out that, as a foreign lawyer, you will be an asset to the firm. If the interviewers bring up the fact that they have foreign clients, describe enthusiastically how you could help with those cases. But do not proactively ask if the firm has any clients in your home country. If your interviewer does not know the answer, you will put him on the spot. Furthermore, do not over-emphasize your desire to do international work! Only discuss it with large firms, which have foreign clients and are involved in cross-border transactions. Do not stress it during your interviews with small or regional mid-size firms, which may want you to practice more traditional areas of law.

Tailor Your Message

U.S. employers routinely recruit foreign attorneys, especially East Coast offices of large firms. Many of these employers are familiar with foreign educational and legal systems. Nevertheless, some employers may have no idea how things work in your home country. They may not know whether your foreign law degree is an undergraduate or a post-graduate degree, whether you went to a prestigious school, or whether your grades and experience measure up to those of your American colleagues. So it is important to tailor your resume and your answers to this audience.

> During her interview with a New York firm, Anna mentioned her clerkship with a court in her home country. "Oh, we have many former clerks here," replied the interviewer. Little did the interviewer know that Anna's clerkship position was so prestigious and difficult to get that it could only be compared to a Supreme Court clerkship here in the States. This was when Anna realized she needed to be more explicit in describing her credentials.

Do not assume that just because you went to one of the most prestigious schools in your country, your interviewers are going to know this. Unless they consistently interview foreign candidates, your interviewers may not be aware of what constitutes a prestigious school or position in your home country. So if you were involved in highly publicized cases, worked at a top-ranked firm, went to a prestigious school, have unique work experience, or received a prestigious award, explain what it means by offering specific details to back up your assertions. For the same reason, consider including law school rankings and an explanation of the grading system along with your resume.

Likewise, do not use foreign terminology or jargon that may be unfamiliar to U.S. employers. Instead of saying you were "called" to the Canadian bar, say that you were "admitted"; note that you wrote legal briefs rather than "factums"; and define "articling year" in terms your interviewer can understand. Conduct online research and speak to foreign lawyers practicing in the States to figure out which phrases and names will be foreign to your interviewers, and use their U.S. equivalents instead.

Immigration Laws

U.S. employment and immigration laws make it more burdensome to hire job applicants born outside the United States. Some larger U.S. employers minimize this burden by hiring in-house lawyers to handle work visas and immigration paperwork for new hires. The majority of legal employers, however, expect candidates to obtain a work permit on their own. Because of the cost and time involved, employers are often hesitant to help foreign attorneys with their immigration papers. Moreover, when interviewing two equally qualified applicants, they may favor the candidate who does not require a work permit. Accordingly, do not initiate discussions about visa issues during an interview, but be prepared to demonstrate that you can easily solve the problem on your own.

An interview is not the right time or place to bring up visa issues. Most interviewers are not familiar enough with these issues to ask the right questions; moreover, they are unlikely to hold your immigration status against you if they are unaware there are issues in the first place. Human resources personnel and recruiting managers are better equipped to address these issues. You may discuss any issues with them during your second or third callback interview, but do not ask for help with your immigration papers during your first interview. There are two reasons for this: first, it may come off as presumptuous if you ask too early in the hiring process; second, you may discourage the employer from hiring you before they even get to know you. That said, it is equally detrimental to wait until after receiving an offer because it may make you look dishonest. Initiate discussions about visas after you know that the employer clearly likes you and most likely wants to hire you, but before you actually get an offer.

Being well-versed in your visa options is crucial. First, your job search will be easier if you know that applicants from your home country who have offers from U.S. employers are eligible for automatic or expedited work visas. Second, it can help you to educate concerned employers who do not know enough about the process. Third, being knowledgeable can help you convince your interviewers that hiring you will not be a burden. Therefore, know what kind of visas you are eligible for, how long it will take to get them, and how much it will cost. If the employers ask, be prepared to present all the options to them.

If an interviewer (rather than an HR representative) initiates a discussion about visas, remember to keep your answers brief and very general, and point out that the process is very easy. To improve your chances even further, consider mentioning that you would be willing to commit to staying with them long term if they help you with your visa documents. Realize, however, that you will have to absorb the costs if the employer refuses to foot the bill.

Cultural Barriers

Because more and more legal employers in the United States are hiring foreign candidates, it is unlikely that you will encounter stereotypes and insensitive questions during your interviews. On rare occasions, however, they do come up. Be prepared to address them by reading Chapter 12 to help you find the right solution. Never judge a firm by an interviewer's questions; one person is not necessarily representative of the firm's culture as a whole. To lighten the mood, consider putting a positive spin on any negative or questionable comments.

> When an interviewer asked Ella about her strong ac-
> cent, Ella replied, "Yes, I am often told I have an accent. It's
> probably very mixed, as I speak three languages. I actually
> have four passports, so I can travel on short notice if the job
> requires it." Ella's ability to spin a challenging question into a
> positive interview story helped her get the job.

Focus on similarities rather than differences. For example, when discussing your work experience, address the similarities between the two legal systems while also emphasizing that you will be quick to learn any differences. When discussing the legal education in your home country, tell the interviewer how it prepared you for practice in the United States. Likewise, when addressing questions about cultural differences, point out the things both cultures have in common. You can even enliven a dry interview by telling your interviewer an interesting story about your home country. This is where cultural differences can work to your advantage. Be receptive to questions about your culture, exchange a few phrases in your native tongue if the interviewer speaks it, and share a tidbit of information your interviewer may not know. Ultimately, do not let cultural differences stand in the way of your job prospects. If your culture or personality makes you feel hesitant to talk about yourself, practice doing so in front of the mirror and with your friends. Your interviewing success depends in large part on your ability to promote your skills and accomplishments. To this end, you may find Chapter 6 helpful.

Finally, be media-savvy. There is nothing worse than being asked about recent elections in your home country and telling the interviewer you have no idea what he or she is talking about. Brush up on current events both in the United States and abroad. Review American news articles about your home country to help you prepare for possible questions.

When interviewing with U.S. employers, try to sound engaging, convincing, and passionate about working in the United States. First and foremost, you must convince your interviewers that you are looking to live and work in the United States long-term (unless they are considering you for a position in their overseas office). Additionally, you need to focus on cultural similarities and emphasize how your unique experience makes you an ideal fit for the job. Finally, be well-versed in U.S. employment and immigration laws so you can easily tackle questions about your visa status.

QuickReview

✓ Prepare a good answer to the "why" question; discuss your ties to the area, your desire to relocate, and reasons for leaving your home country.

✓ Tailor your background, experience, and credentials to U.S. employers, and avoid unfamiliar jargon and terminology.

✓ Brush up on news and current events.

✓ Emphasize your language skills and unique experience, and explain how they will benefit the employer.

✓ Do not bring up visa issues prematurely in the interviewing process, and only discuss them with the right people.

✓ Be aware of cultural barriers, but use them to your advantage.

Index

ᥰ᥊᥊ᥲᥩ

A

AbovetheLaw.com, 111

alcohol at meal interviews, 122

American Corporate Counsel Association, 33

application stand out, how to make your, 151-152

attire, appropriate interviewing, 43

awkward moments, gap-fillers for, 83-86

B

background check, 167-168

beer, offering your interviewer a, 98

body language in interviewing, 61-62

bold moves in interviews, 97-100

bonus, start date's effect on year-end, 205

briefcase to take to an interview, type of, 49

business casual, 45

C

callback interview expenses, 138-139

callback interviews,
not letting your guard down during, 137-138
send thank-you letters for, 139-140
when to schedule a, 25

callback stage at larger firms, 31

career counselors, 146

career goals during a lateral interview, discussing, 170

chambers, when it is okay to call the, 152-153

clerkship interview,
preparing for a, 153-154
questions you may ask during a, 156-157
topics and questions during, 154-155

clerkship interviews, 151-158
gathering information for, 32
timing of, 153
when to schedule, 26

clerkship offer, responding to a, 157-158

ABOUT THE AUTHORS

Natalie Prescott joined a major international firm in San Diego, California, following a federal clerkship. She holds a BA, summa cum laude, from the University of Southern Mississippi; an MA from Tulane University; and a JD, cum laude, from Duke University School of Law. Previously, she worked as a journalist in Europe. Her recent awards and honors include being named as one of San Diego's best young attorneys, and receiving the California Bar Association 2008 Jack Berman Achievement Award for her contributions to the legal community and the public. In addition to numerous publications and speaking engagements, she volunteers as a career counselor and mock interviewer at several law schools, serves on the Duke alumni admissions interviewing committee, and frequently speaks on job-related topics.

Oleg Cross is an attorney with a national firm in San Diego, California. He holds a BA, magna cum laude, from Abilene Christian University, and a JD and LLM from Duke University School of Law. He frequently writes and speaks on various emerging legal issues. In 2007 and 2008, Mr. Cross was named one of San Diego's best young attorneys—the "brightest up-and-coming players in the San Diego legal community." Having interviewed numerous applicants for law firm positions, he now volunteers as a career counselor for his alma mater, serves on the Duke alumni admissions interviewing committee, and provides career coaching to young attorneys.